Burial Ledger
of
St. Elizabeths Hospital
Washington, D.C.

July 5, 1917-August 30, 1983

Paul E. Sluby, Sr.

HERITAGE BOOKS
2008

HERITAGE BOOKS

AN IMPRINT OF HERITAGE BOOKS, INC.

Books, CDs, and more—Worldwide

For our listing of thousands of titles see our website
at
www.HeritageBooks.com

Published 2008 by
HERITAGE BOOKS, INC.
Publishing Division
100 Railroad Ave. #104
Westminster, Maryland 21157

Cover Photo: Center building at St. Elizabeths Hospital
Source: St. Elizabeths Hospital

International Standard Book Numbers
Paperbound: 978-0-7884-4903-1
Clothbound: 978-0-7884-7498-9

CONTENTS

INTRODUCTION

Early records that contain vital data on individuals are very important to those engaged in demography and sociology but, in particular, to genealogists. Whether engaged as a professional or layman, the daunting and time-consuming task to uncover ancestors is based on basic and as much original information on a forefather that can be found. Essential in this regard are records that contain the date of birth or death, but ideally, both. Cemetery records are one of several sources that help fill this information gap and often prove a lifesaver in the absence of official documentation.

For the most part, State offices maintain vital records dating from the early twentieth century. Locally, however, these reports date from the mid to late nineteenth century. In nearby Virginia, the State office maintains birth and death records dating from 1853 until 1896, and do not begin again until 1912. In the District of Columbia a *Register of Deaths* was started in 1855 in which some deaths were recorded for a short time. During the Civil War years (1861-1865), though, no official vital records of any type were kept in the city. Birth records are available from 1874. In Maryland, these records for Baltimore city are available from 1875, but State records date from 1898. Births and deaths that occurred during these initial periods may not have been reported at all and, even when made public, the particulars are only as accurate as the memory of the informant.

In addition to providing vital dates that were recorded at a given facility at the time the event occurred, the contents of the burials records published in this volume offer additional and extraordinary details. The reasons why many people became patients at St. Elizabeths ranged from emotional trauma to physical attributes. The nicknames and aliases sometimes provided offer a deeper look at the individual concerned. The broad ethnic disparity suggests that the subsequent atmosphere may have promoted a city within a city for many of the patients.

Through the passage of time, records once diligently maintained often disappear. Some unreplaceable ledgers become filled to capacity and are placed in an out-of-the-way place for safekeeping. Years later, when the urge strikes to "throw out the old stuff," or during a renovation project, books and anything else unfamiliar are discarded. The St. Elizabeths burial ledger was saved from this fate. We are indeed fortunate that this valuable historical reference source has been preserved.

Paul E. Sluby, Sr.

ST. ELIZABETHS HOSPITAL

BRIEF HISTORY

The "Government Hospital for the Insane" was founded in Washington, D.C., on March 3, 1855. According to Dorothy Dix, who wrote the bill establishing the institution, its purpose was to provide "the most humane care and enlightened curative treatment of the insane of the Army and Navy and of the United States and of the District of Columbia."[1] Located in the southeast section of the city, the hospital is situated on a hill that affords a panoramic view of the Anacostia and Potomac rivers. Its grounds are divided by Martin Luther King, Jr. Avenue forming an East Campus and a West Campus.[2] In 1916, the name was officially changed to St. Elizabeths (with the apostrophe omitted) in response to recovering soldiers who disliked reference to "Insane."

During its opening years its first superintendent, Dr. Charles H. Nichols, established the initial procedural directives and oversaw the construction of several buildings. Among those erected were the Center (administration) Building, the West and East Wing patient areas, and the West and East lodges. These accommodations and the application of the most modern medical knowledge thrusted St. Elizabeths to the forefront in the treatment of the mentally ill during that time. At the onset of the Civil War (1861-1865), however, the facility was used for extensive military purposes. As the war progressed the need arose to quickly and conveniently treat the wounded and St. Elizabeths was a favored choice because of its closeness to Washington and its many facilities. A Signal Corp unit was located there as were the Navy General and Quarantine Hospital and the Union General Hospital. In addition, an artificial limb manufacturing shop existed there from 1863 until May 31, 1864.[3]

BURIAL AREAS

Several burial areas were established on the hospital grounds to accommodate the thousands of civilian and military patients who died at St. Elizabeths from 1856 until 1983.[4] These include one (1) cemetery on the West Campus and three (3) cemeteries on the East Campus.

---

[1] U.S. Congress, Title LIX, Section 4838, Establishment of the Government Hospital for the Insane, 33rd Congress, March 3, 1855.

[2] The hospital address is 2700 Martin Luther King, Jr. Avenue, SE, Washington, D.C. 20020.

[3] Dr. Suryabala Kanhouva and Dr. Jogues R. Prandoni, "The Civil War and St. Elizabeths Hospital: An Untold Story of Services from the First Federal Mental Institution in the United States." The Journal of Civil War Medicine, Vol. 9, No. 1 (Jan./Feb./Mar. 2005), p. 3.

[4] After 1983 the remains of those dying at the hospital either were buried by the surviving family at a chosen cemetery or, for indigents, buried in an unspecified District cemetery at public expense.

West Campus Cemetery: Resting on a hillside facing Interstate 295 is a burial area that was first utilized about 1856 for the burial of general patients.[5] In 1864, and for several years thereafter, many Civil War casualties also were interred here. This included Union and Confederate soldiers and other military personnel who were buried adjacent to each other, without distinction to affiliation or ethnicity. This cemetery was closed in 1873. Today, it is fronted with a modern stone wall having an attached commemorative plaque.

East Campus Cemeteries: There are three cemeteries located in the far eastern portion of the East Campus. These, individually, are dedicated to the burial of Army personnel, Navy and Marine personnel, and General Patients. The transcribed burial ledger presented in this book is a partial record of those deceased patients interred in the General Patients area.

GENERAL PATIENTS CEMETERY

After space in the West Campus area was exhausted the burial of general patients in this east side location commenced about 1873. Shown in an aerial view on the following page, this burial ground is east of the John Howard Pavilion and appears as an unutilized field. This is vastly different from the dedicated military burial areas which contain many hundreds of neatly lined military markers that identify the deceased. In the General Patients area are found only the headstone for Fred Goldstein, a small stone inscribed with "Baby Joe, aged 3 years," and two (2) ground flush markers, one for George Dahrooge and another for Louis R. Wolfes.

Burial Density

The location of the initial sites utilized to open this cemetery in 1873 is unknown. Upon official development of the area in the early twentieth century, however, the cemetery was laid out in Sections 28-42.[6] There were 2,264 planned graves covering 28,800 square feet.

DESCRIPTION OF THE LEDGER

Acquisition

The St. Elizabeths Burial Ledger, personally salvaged several years ago from material being destroyed during renovation activity at the hospital, is about 8" x 14" in size. Handwritten, it contains a fairly accurate index. The original ledger is in the hands of Michael G. Rhode.[7] A photocopy of the

---

[5] The term "general patients" refers to civilians as well as former military personnel who remained at the hospital after their service commitment.

[6] The abutting military burial area ended with Section 27.

[7] Michael G. Rhode is Chief Archivist, National Museum of Health and Medicine, Armed Forces Institute of Pathology, Walter Reed Army Medical Center, Washington, D.C.

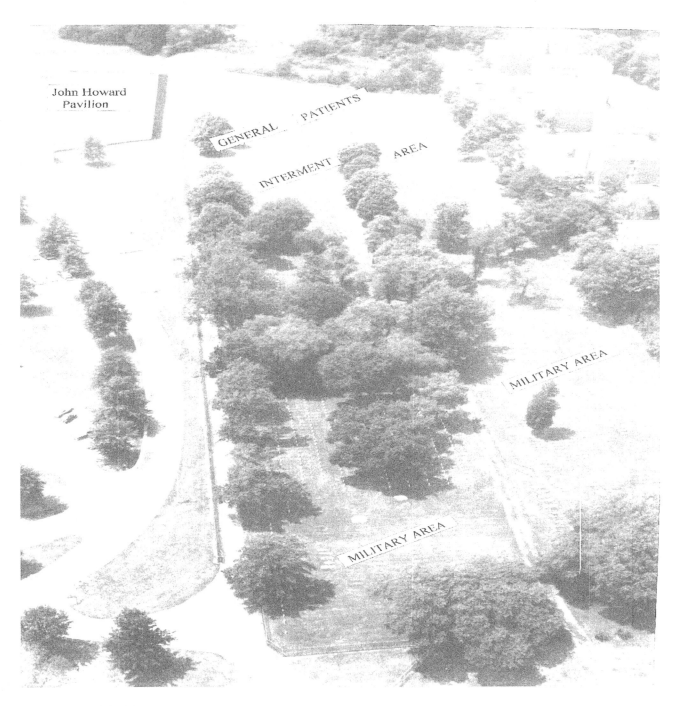

John Howard
Pavilion

GENERAL PATIENTS

INTERMENT AREA

MILITARY AREA

MILITARY AREA

Photo: Personal Archives

Aerial view of a portion of the East Campus Cemetery area. Two military areas appear at the left and right bottom of the picture. The General Patients interment area is the open field at the top beyond the center grove of trees, adjacent to the right of the wall of the John Howard Pavalion.

ledger is available at the Martin Luther King, Jr. Library, Washingtoniana Room, Washington, D.C.

Ledger Contents

The Hospital burial ledger, dating from 1917-1983, contains over 2,900 entries regarding burials of the general patient population. In addition to providing the name, age, death date, cause of death, and grave location, there are occasional notations that provide important details about the deceased. Sometimes corrections to an entry are included that provide important details, such as an alias or nickname. References to heritage also may be entered, such as "Indian," "colored man," "Japanese," or "Chinese." Occasionally, the word "Exhumed" appears, which indicates the remains were removed to another location. Enlightening facts also surface, such as the reference to William Powell Jenkins, who died on February 27, 1931 and was buried "between graves." In another instance, it is noted that John T. McRand was "Buried first in Arlington Nat'l Cem. In Va. Exhumed and reburied in Hosp. Cem."

As enumerated below, the remains of a number of Native Americans, referred to as "Indian" in the ledger, and Prisoners lie in this cemetery:

Native Americans

Bessie Rising Sun
Charles Creeping
Charles LaCompte
Charlie
Fidel Vigil
Francisco Zuna
Frank Bear
Hoskee Yazzie
Kate Canoe
Mabel Tsinnyinnie

Meda Ensign
Neska
Priscilla Benally
Rado Miletich
Richard Fair Bank
Robert Jackson
Samuel White
Sarah Short Norman
Strikes On Top

Prisoners

Anderson, Sam
Andrewshck, John
Barnes, Charlie
Burgess, John
Burton, Frank L.
Heido, August S.
Ivry, Luis
Kelty, William E.
Mann, Joe
Matchett, William H.

Manzer, Bert
Newman, B.
O'Connell, John
Plunkett, Robert P.
Rhodes, Eliza L.
Rigo, Tony
Rood, Peter
Stempen, John
White, Onarie G.
Zaishoff, Charles

4

TRANSCRIBING PROCESS

General: Although there is one instance in the ledger that burial information dates from 1914,[8] the primary entries range from July 5, 1917 to August 30, 1983. Different handwriting throughout the document suggests it was maintained by several individuals. Pages 50 and 51 are missing in the original ledger.

Columned Information: From the initial entry until July 14, 1930, the columned information is confined to the Name, Dates of Death and Burial, and the Section, Site and Grave Number utilized for the interment. Subsequently, columns were added to include Race, Sex, and Cause of Death.[9]

Supplemental Notes: Occasionally, apparent corrections to names or other additions accompany an entry. These items are sometimes written haphazardly or appears in parenthesis. During the transcribing process, data of this type appear in the "Remarks" column with cross-indexing added to accommodate name changes, an alias or a nickname.

---

[8] Alfred Horton is enumerated in 1914.

[9] The "Cause of Death" information is not included in the printed transcription.

LAST NAME	FIRST NAME	MIDDLE	DIED	INTERRED	SEC.	ROW	GRAVE	G	R	REMARKS
Abbs	E. Y.	Mattie								
Abolin	Edgar									
Abribet	Joseph									See: Arbebettor, Joseph
Acton	Marcellus		1925 Jan 20	1925 Jan 23	23	5	1217			
Acton	Venus		1934 Apr 25	1934 May 2	28	5	119A	M	C	
Acuna	Santiago		1921 Jun 9	1921 Jun 10	3	10	1753			
Adams	Daniel		1935 May 3	1935 May 8	29	2	195A	M	C	
Adams	Emily		1917 Dec 23	1917 Dec 27	25	5	1723			
Adams	James	B.								
Adams	John									
Adams	Lillian									
Adams	Vernon	A.								
Addis	Wellford		1936 May 31	1936 Jun 2	29	3	211A	M	W	
Adriaane	John	H.								
Ages	Morris									
Air	Thomas									
Aitkins	Cordelia									
Albans	Frank		1918 Nov 15	1918 Nov 19	22	5	1206			
Alberdi	Felipi		1935 Sep 3	1935 Sep 10	29	2	179A	M	W	
Albert	Jesy									
Albyne	Richard		1919 Jan 11	1919 Jan 15	18	5	1088			
Alderson	Charles									
Alderson	Rose		1932 Jan 28	1932 Feb 2	21	1	1607	F	C	
Alexander	Anthony									
Alexander	Bell		1929 Feb 15	1929 Feb 21	20	4	1253			
Alexander	Herbert									
Alexander	Jane		1935 Oct 1	1935 Oct 8	21	4	1269	F	C	
Alexander	Keller									
Alexander	Nathan		1926 Mar 22	1926 Mar 26	19	1	680			
Alexander	Wille									
Alexandrine	Jacobs									
Alfred	Charles									
Allen	Charles	E.	1928 Oct 18	1928 Oct 23	19	4	1011			
Allen	Fred									
Allen	Grace		1930 Feb 6	1930 Feb 12	20	5	1138			
Allen	Harry	C.								
Allen	James									
Allen	John		1926 Jan 15	1926 Jan 22	15	1	113			
Allen	Mattie		1933 Aug 4	1933 Aug 8	21	4	1490	F	C	

LAST NAME	FIRST NAME	MIDDLE	DIED	INTERRED	SEC.	ROW	GRAVE	G	R	REMARKS
Allen	Oden	J.								
Allen	Reginard									
Allen	Rome									
Allen	Rose									
Allen	Virgie	M.								
Allen	William		1934 Aug 27	1934 Aug 30	29	1	167A	M		
Alley	E.	R.	1919 Mar 25	1919 Mar 29	23	1	1678			
Alphonse	M.		1918 May 12	1918 May 14	22	4	1304			Alias: Morille, A.
Alston	Edith	M.								
Alvis	Emma									
Amer	Joe									(Armond); Indian
Amity	Gertrude	C.								
Andeerson	Morris									
Anderson	A.	N.								
Anderson	Betsy									
Anderson	Clarence		1919 Nov 6	1919 Nov 8	22	2	1522			
Anderson	Delos		1931 Feb 19	1931 Feb 26	28	2	53A	M	W	
Anderson	Eric		1924 Dec 2	1924 Dec 5	23	5	1214			
Anderson	Ernest	R.		1922 Jun 26	23	3	1453			Body removed by T. Hanlon.
Anderson	Francis	R.								
Anderson	Howard	F.								
Anderson	James									
Anderson	James									
Anderson	James	W.								
Anderson	John		1919 Mar 1	1919 Mar 6	23	1	1675			
Anderson	Julious		1936 May 20					F	W	
Anderson	Lelia	A.	1933 Apr 26	1933 May 3	28	4	108A	M	C	
Anderson	Louis									
Anderson	Nellie	L.								
Anderson	Peter		1928 Dec 1	1928 Dec 8	19	4	1018			
Anderson	Robert	L.								
Anderson	Sally									
Anderson	Sam		1932 Aug 1	1932 Aug 8	28	3	79A	M	C	U. S. Prisoner
Anderson	Seymour		1926 Aug 16	1926 Aug 23	19	2	784			
Anderson	Thomas									
Anderson	William									
Andrews	Jessie		1918 Mar 16	1918 Mar 19	22	4	1300			
Andrewshak	John		1934 Apr 2	1934 Apr 9	28	5	122A	M		
Angel	Mary	Ann	1919 Jan 21	1919 Jan 25	20	1	1577		W	D. C. Prisoner

LAST NAME	FIRST NAME	MIDDLE	DIED	INTERRED	SEC.	ROW	GRAVE	G	R	REMARKS
Angle	Murrell									
Antisdale	Asa	H.	1936 Feb 13	1936 Feb 20	29	3	225A	M	W	
Apodoca	Tony									
Arana	Jose									
Arbebettor	Joseph									Alias: Arbitt; (Abribet)
Arbitt	Joseph		1926 Apr 9	1926 Apr 14	19	1	684			See: Arbebettor, Joseph
Armond	Joe									See: Amer, Joe
Armstead	Lee									
Armstrong	John									
Arnn	Lloyd		1936 Jun 21	1936 Jun 16	21	4	1288	M	W	
Arosehin	Caroline	W.	1917 Oct 4	1917 Oct 8	25	5	1718			
Ashby	John	L.								
Ashcraft	David									
Ashland	Nellie									
Ashley	Jenrette									
Ashton	Harrison		1937 Dec 15	1937 Dec 21	29	5	262A	M	C	
Ashton	John		1921 Oct 1	1921 Oct 5	23	3	1443			
Ashton	William	J.								
Ashwander	Gottlieb		1926 Jan 25	1926 Jan 30	19	1	671			
Asplund	Martin		1926 Jun 1	1926 Jun 3	19	1	688			
Aston	Robert	A.								
Atkins	William									
Atwood	Charles		1921 Jun 29	1921 Jul 2	15	1	98			
Atwood	Harry									
Augusta	Joanna		1935 Jul 24	1935 Jul 29	21	3	1395	F	W	
Aureden	Flora									
Aurelio	V.	Erum								
Austin	Fannie		1919 Apr 15	1919 Apr 19	20	1	1580			
Austin	Mary									
Austin	William									
Avedon	Mollie									
Bachelor	James	M.								
Backer	Lief		1920 May 10	1920 May 13	15	1	93			
Bacon	Willie									
Badne	John									
Bagwell	Frank									
Bailey	Charles									See: Baylor, Charles
Baker	Benjamin	L.	1917 Sep 13	1917 Sep 17	18	3	878			
Baker	Blanche		1919 Jan 12	1919 Jan 14	20	1	1574			

LAST NAME	FIRST NAME	MIDDLE	DIED	INTERRED	SEC.	ROW	GRAVE	G	R	REMARKS
Baker	Charles	H.								
Baker	James		1929 May 11	1929 May 16	20	4	1262			
Baker	Martha									
Baker	Natalia									
Baker	Sophie									
Baker	Walten									
Bakonyi	Andrew									
Bakuis	Jacobus		1935 Jun 23	1935 Jun 26	29	2	187A	M	W	
Baldin	Pinkney		1918 Oct 17	1918 Oct 21	22	5	1194			
Baldwin	Clarence	W.								
Baldwin	James									
Balk	Frances		1921 Mar 4	1921 Mar 7	20	2	1454			
Ball	Marvin									
Ball	William	A.	1933 Dec 30	1934 Jan 6	28	5	137A	M	W	
Ballinger	Andrew		1918 Jan 19	1918 Jan 22	22	4	1294			
Bamman	Frederick									
Banks	Delia									
Banks	Jake									
Banks	Mary		1937 Jul 3	1937 Jul 8	21	5	1173	F	C	
Bara	Victor	E.								
Barbey	Elizabeth									
Barker	Joseph									
Barker	Margaret									
Barner	Frank									
Barnes	Annie									
Barnes	Charlie									D. C. Prisoner
Barnes	Cynthia									See: Burns, Cynthia
Barnes	Ida									
Barnett	William									
Barnette	Rosetta									
Baron	Glaya									
Baron	L.		1917 Dec 4	1917 Dec 7	22	4	1290			
Barreett	Kate		1933 Nov 8	1933 Nov 15	21	4	1495	F	C	
Barron	Cornelia	C.	1930 Oct 2	1930 Oct 13	20	5	1147	F	C	
Barrow	Samuel	W.								
Barry	John	E.	1920 Feb 10	1920 Feb 12	23	3	1426			Berry
Barton	Mary	A.								
Bassett	William									
Bateman	Mary	N.	1918 Jul 6	1918 Jul 10	25	5	1735			

LAST NAME	FIRST NAME	MIDDLE	DIED	INTERRED	SEC.	ROW	GRAVE	G	R	REMARKS
Bateman	William									
Batmer	Peter		1931 Aug 9	1931 Aug 14	28	2	41A	M	W	
Bauer	Peter									See: Bauner, Peter
Baugardes	Anna		1933 Jun 27	1933 Jul 3	21	4	1489	F	W	
Baurner	Peter		1919 May 18	1919 May 20	23	2	1540			(Bauer)
Baxter	Ella		1919 Oct 1	1919 Oct 3	20	1	1585			
Bayard	Edward									
Baylor	Charles		1929 Mar 12	1929 Mar 18	19	5	1104			Alias: Bailey
Bean	Anna									
Bean	Joseph		1923 Sep 17	1923 Sep 22	23	4	1333			
Beany	Nichael									See: By, Nichael
Bear	Frank									Indian
Beard	Kate									
Beck	Martha									
Beckman	Theodore									
Bedmute	Philipe		1918 Jan 7	1918 Jan 10	22	4	1293			
Bednorski	Joseph									
Behan	Lawrence									
Beijer	Frank		1930 Aug 6	1930 Aug 12	28	1	10A	M	W	
Bell	Benjamin									
Bell	Clara	A.								
Bell	Edward		1924 Aug 23	1924 Aug 27	23	5	1213			
Bell	Elizabeth									
Bell	Gertrude	P.	1934 Jan 8	1934 Jan 12	21	4	1497	F	W	
Bell	John									
Bell	Joseph	E.	1924 Mar 30	1924 Apr 1	22	5	Between			Bet. 1198 & 99; not a patient.
Bell	Mary		1918 Jun 27	1918 Jul 1	25	5	1734			
Bell	Ogle	G.	1935 Feb 25	1935 Mar 4	29	1	147A	M	C	
Bell	Sadie									
Bell	William		1927 Mar 30	1927 Apr 4	19	3	894			
Belle	Lockey									See: Lockey, Belle
Bells	Ella									
Benally	Priscilla									
Bench	Alex									Indian
Bender	Harry	B.								
Benedick	Mike		1921 Nov 17	1921 Nov 22	23	3	1444			
Benjamin	Mabel									
Benjamin	Viola									
Benlay	Frank	W.								

LAST NAME	FIRST NAME	MIDDLE	DIED	INTERRED	SEC.	ROW	GRAVE	G	R	REMARKS
Bennett	Mary		1934 Aug 20	1934 Aug 23	21	4	1509	F	W	
Bennett	Sarah		1932 Aug 13	1932 Aug 18	21	5	1618	F	W	
Benson	Jennie									
Benson	Sarah									
Berberham	George	J.								
Bergin	Mary		1922 Mar 14	1922 Mar 17	20	2	1459			
Bergman	Charles	G.	1925 Nov 8	1925 Nov 10	23	5	1236			See: Berrigan, Susan (Sarah)
Berrigan	Sarah									
Berrigan	Susan		1922 Mar 21	1922 Mar 24	20	2	1460			
Berry	Esther		1931 Mar 3	1931 Mar 9	20	5	1156	F	C	See: Barry, John
Berry	John									
Berry	Mable		1926 Mar 20	1926 Mar 24	20	3	1345			
Berry	Maria		1917 Oct 30	1917 Nov 1	25	5	1722			
Berry	Mary	A.								
Best	Rupert	E.								
Bethea	Cecelia	H.								
Bethelerny	Charlotte									See: Betherny, Charlotte (Bethelerny)
Betherny	Charlotte		1918 Mar 17	1918 Mar 19	25	5	1727			
Betts	Andrew									
Beverly	William		1926 Dec 6	1926 Dec 9	19	2	801			
Biedler	Charles	M.	1919 Sep 27	1919 Oct 1	23	2	1550			
Biggs	William	A.								
Bigonness	Jack	C.								
Biscope	Wesley		1918 Sep 15	1918 Sep 18	22	5	1187			
Bishop	Willard		1935 Apr 13	1935 Apr 18	21	3	1387	F	W	
Bixler	Mamie									
Black	James									
Blackistone	Richard		1936 Apr 2	1936 Apr 7	29	3	221A	M	C	
Blackouski	John									
Blackstone	Jarmiah		1918 Jul 30	1918 Aug 1	22	4	1311			(Jeremiah)
Blackstone	Jeremiah									See: Blackstone, Jarmiah
Blackstone	John		1926 Jul 7	1926 Jul 10	10	1	694			
Blackwell	Robert									
Blair	Robert		1930 May 29	1930 Jun 4	28	1	18A			
Blake	Ellen									
Blake	William	A.								
Bland	Lillian									
Blocker	Clara									
Blocker	Clarence									

LAST NAME	FIRST NAME	MIDDLE	DIED	INTERRED	SEC.	ROW	GRAVE	G	R	REMARKS
Bloomguist	Haagan		1926 Jul 21	1926 Jul 27	3	19	1747			
Blount	Oits									
Blue	Furman	H.								
Blurm	Jacob		1919 May 20	1919 May 23	18	5	1102			
Bobcock	Llewelyn									
Bodden	Adam									
Bodden	Lizzie	Hicken	1920 Oct 28	1920 Oct 30	20	1	1595			
Bohaczek	Presley									
Bohnson	Christian		1917 Dec 22	1917 Dec 26	18	3	885			
Bolden	Anna									
Bolton	Marey	B.								
Bomar	Samuel									
Bonelli	Harry	E.								
Bongers	George									
Booker	Mary	M. J.								
Boone	Serah									
Boone	Thomas		1929 Nov 18	1929 Nov 21	19	5	1124			
Bordugowsky	Maria									
Bosnak	Joseph									
Bosse	John									
Boston	Andrew		1920 Feb 22	1920 Feb 25	23	3	1428			
Boswell	Philip		1919 Nov 21	1919 Nov 24	23	2	1552			
Botts	Edith	B.								
Botts	Maggie									
Bourman	H.	Ellen	1933 Apr 3	1933 Apr 7	21	4	1483	F	C	
Bovi	Joseph		1919 Dec 2	1919 Dec 5	23	2	1553			
Bowers	Alfred									
Bowers	Nettie	L.								
Bowie	B.	Stanton								
Bowie	Elmira		1935 Dec 3	1935 Dec 19	21	4	1274	F	C	
Bowie	George		1918 Sep 20	1918 Sep 24	22	5	1188			
Bowley	Adeline									
Bowman	Alexander									
Bowman	Charles	H.								
Bowman	Fred									
Bowman	Letha	L.								
Bowman	Mary	E.								
Boxley	Archie		1935 Aug 4	1935 Aug 8	29	2	182A	M	C	
Boyce	Rosa									

LAST NAME	FIRST NAME	MIDDLE	DIED	INTERRED	SEC.	ROW	GRAVE	G	R	REMARKS
Boyd	James									
Bradley	William	E.	1918 Oct 25	1918 Oct 28	18	4	997			
Bradshaw	Samuel									Exhumed
Brady	Georgiania									
Bramble	James		1935 May 17	1935 May 22	29	2	193A	M	W	
Brand	Charles	M.	1935 May 25	1935 May 31	29	2	192A	M	W	
Brandau	Irene									See: Brandor, Irene (Brandau)
Brandor	Irene		1918 Nov 20	1918 Nov 26	20	1	1569			
Brandt	Bertha									
Brandt	Chifford									
Branson	Frank									
Branson	Harry									
Breazeale	Dorothy	L.								
Breck	Charles		1929 May 20	1929 May 27	19	5	1109			
Breen	Elizabeth	M.								
Brenner	John									
Brent	Richrd									
Brent	William		1919 Jul 13	1919 Jul 16	23	2	1544			
Bressie	Clara									
Brewster	Ernest									
Briagman	Edward									
Bridaham	Henry									
Bridges	Joe		1919 Jan 12	1919 Jan 15	23	1	1666			
Bridgett	Winston									
Briggs	Carrie									
Briggs	Julia		1926 Jun 29	1926 Jul 1	20	3	1349			
Briggs	Rosa		1932 Jun 21	1932 Jun 25	21	5	1615	F	C	Alias: Eidler
Brink	Evelyn									
Briscoe	George	A.								
Britts	Joseph	E.								See: Doe, John
Broadus	L.	Russell								
Brockenburg	Amanda									
Brockman	James									
Bronaugh	Willie	D.								
Brooks	Bernard		1935 Mar 16	1935 Mar 20	29	2	203A	M	C	
Brooks	Casey		1928 Jan 26	1928 Jan 31	19	3	918			
Brooks	Clarence									
Brooks	Earnest	M.								
Brooks	Frances									

LAST NAME	FIRST NAME	MIDDLE	DIED	INTERRED	SEC.	ROW	GRAVE	G	R	REMARKS
Brooks	Jennie									
Brown	Ada									
Brown	Archie	L.	1917 Jul 19	1917 Jul 23	18	3	875			
Brown	Arnold									
Brown	Berle		1937 Aug 19	1937 Aug 25	29	5	280A	M	C	
Brown	Bertha									
Brown	Bessie		1929 Nov 30	1929 Dec 7	20	5	1136			
Brown	Bessie									
Brown	Buren		1926 Mar 12	1926 Mar 17	19	1	677			
Brown	Carrie		1930 Apr 16	1930 Apr 22	20	5	1141			
Brown	Charles	P.								
Brown	Charles									
Brown	Cora									
Brown	Dominick									
Brown	Ester									
Brown	Eugene	G.								
Brown	Florence		1933 Jun 24	1933 Jul 1	21	4	1488	F	W	
Brown	Frank		1921 Feb 5	1921 Feb 8	23	3	1434			
Brown	Frank									
Brown	George									
Brown	Henry	T.								
Brown	Henry	J.								
Brown	James									
Brown	James		1925 Jul 23	1925 Jul 28	23	5	1233			
Brown	James	P.								
Brown	John		1919 Jan 5	1919 Jan 9	18	5	1086			
Brown	Josephine									
Brown	Joshua									
Brown	Lizzie									
Brown	Lula									
Brown	Mary	R.	1918 Feb 21	1918 Feb 25	25	5	1726			
Brown	Mary									
Brown	Matilda									
Brown	Millie		1925 Mar 10	1925 Mar 13	20	2	1471			
Brown	Nathaniel									
Brown	Nellie									
Brown	Raymond	H.								
Brown	Rebecca									
Brown	Sam									

LAST NAME	FIRST NAME	MIDDLE	DIED	INTERRED	SEC.	ROW	GRAVE	G	R	REMARKS
Brown	Susie									
Brown	Sylvester									
Brown	Walter		1928 Jan 28	1928 Feb 5	19	4	1023			
Brown	William	C.								Alias: Vandyne
Brown	William	F.								
Brown	William		1919 Feb 18	1919 Feb 21	18	5	1092			
Browning	Benj.	F.	1932 Mar 15	1932 Mar 21	28	3	87A	M	W	
Bruce	Eliza	P.								
Bruder	Leo									
Bruegger	Louisa									
Brumby	Richard									See: Bumby, Richard
Brummrett	Clarence	M.								
Bruno	Antonio									
Bryan	Joseph									
Bryan	William	J.	1930 Nov 13	1930 Nov 20	28	1	1A	M	W	
Bryant	Dewey		1926 Mar 23	1926 Mar 30	19	1	681			
Bryant	Frank	B.								
Bryant	Laura	L.								
Buchanan	John		1927 Jun 30	1927 Jul 5	19	3	902			
Buchanan	Mary	J.								
Buckley	Joseph	H.	1918 Oct 16	1918 Oct 18	22	5	1192			
Buckner	Charles	C.								
Buehl	B.	Hannah								
Buffington	Price		1918 Nov 3	1918 Nov 6	22	5	1204			
Buineck	Nicholas		1930 Sep 25	1930 Oct 2	28	1	5A	M	W	
Bumby	Richard		1927 Dec 20	1927 Dec 27	19	3	913			(Brumby)
Bumpers	Thomas									
Burch	Bernard	W.								
Burgess	Issiah		1935 Feb 1	1935 Feb 8	29	1	149A	M	W	U. S. Prisoner
Burgess	John									
Buri	John									
Burke	George		1936 Jan 13	1936 Jan 20	29	3	229A	M	W	
Burke	James		1926 Jan 22	1926 Jan 28	15	1	114			
Burke	Walter	S.								
Burley	Frank									
Burley	Lizzie		1918 Aug 12	1918 Aug 17	25	5	1738			
Burll	Thern		1918 Oct 16	1918 Oct 18	18	4	987			
Burnette	Charlotte		1926 Mar 11	1926 Mar 15	20	3	1343			
Burney	Jean		1936 Mar 15	1936 Mar 19	21	4	1283	F	C	

LAST NAME	FIRST NAME	MIDDLE	DIED	INTERRED	SEC.	ROW	GRAVE	G	R	REMARKS
Burns	Cynthia		1918 Aug 2	1918 Aug 6	25	5	1736		W	(Barnes, Cynthia)
Burns	John	I.	1935 Jul 21	1935 Jul 24	29	2	184A	M	W	
Burns	Mary									
Burns	Robert		1934 Jan 24	1934 Jan 26	28	5	132A	M	W	
Buscher	Phillip	H.								
Bush	Curtis	C.								
Bush	Ernest	D.	1919 Apr 30	1919 May 5	18	5	1099			
Butch	Reddy		1918 Aug 2	1918 Aug 5	22	4	1313			
Butcher	Georgianna									
Butler	Alexander		1927 Feb 7	1927 Feb 14	19	2	808			
Butler	Betty	M.								
Butler	Caroline	R.								
Butler	Charles	H.								
Butler	Cordelia		1929 Dec 4	1929 Dec 4	20	5	1135			
Butler	Edward	H.								
Butler	Elizabeth		1934 Nov 6	1934 Dec 11	21	3	1376	F	C	
Butler	Elizabeth									
Butler	George									
Butler	Henry									
Butler	Issac									
Butler	James	J.								
Butler	James									
Butler	Maria									
Butler	Robert		1919 Feb 27	1919 Mar 4	23	1	1674			
Butler	Virginia									
Butler	William	W.	1934 Jun 1	1934 Jun 6	29	1	173A	M	W	Alias: Beany
By	Nichael									
Byrd	Frances									
Cafferty	John	L.								
Caffery	Helen									
Cahalon	Harry	F.								
Cain	Patric		1919 Dec 22	1919 Dec 26	15	1	92			Alias: Kilby, Thomas
Caldwell	Etta									
Caldwell	William	B.	1927 Aug 7	1927 Aug 11	19	3	904			
Callahan	Belle									
Calloway	Carrie									
Callwood	Gladys									
Cambell	John	H.								
Campbell	Emma		1923 Sep 17	1923 Sep 20	20	2	1463			

LAST NAME	FIRST NAME	MIDDLE	DIED	INTERRED	SEC.	ROW	GRAVE	G	R	REMARKS
Campbell	Hannah	M.								
Campbell	Henry	F.	1936 May 15	1936 May 19	29	3	213A	M	W	
Campbell	Lemuel		1919 Mar 16	1919 Mar 20	23	1	1677			
Campbell	Lena		1928 Dec 20	1928 Dec 20	20	4	1247			
Campbell	Mary									
Campell	Anna									
Canauiski	Joseph		1937 Apr 3	1937 Apr 8	29	4	235A	M	W	
Cancelos	Francesco		1928 Nov 15	1928 Nov 20	19	4	1015			
Cane	Gilbert	W.								
Cannon	John	B.	1919 Jul 15	1919 Jul 19	23	2	1546			
Cannon	Samuel		1929 Dec 28	1930 Jan 2	19	5	1128			
Canoe	Kate									Indian
Cantellyn	Warren	A.								
Carberry	Fredrick	M.	1922 Jun 9	1922 Jun 15	15	1	104			
Carbone	Joe									
Carcom	Mary									
Carey	Lena	M.								
Carloo	Sanker									
Carlos	Anna									
Carokis	Thomas		1918 Oct 20	1918 Oct 23	22	5	1198			
Caroll	Emma		1930 Aug 10	1930 Aug 18	20	5	1144	F	C	
Carpenter	Zelie									
Carr	Annie									
Carr	Edward		1937 Oct 8	1937 Oct 14	29	5	271A	M	W	
Carroll	Florence	D.	1935 May 13	1935 May 16	21	3	1389	F	C	
Carroll	Frances	J.								
Carroll	James									
Carroll	James									(Shea)
Carroll	William		1930 May 3	1930 May 10	28	1	20A			Colored D.C.
Carta	Mike									
Carter	Ada		1928 Jan 19	1928 Jan 19	20	4	1250			
Carter	Carrie									
Carter	Edith									
Carter	Elisbeth		1935 Jul 2	1935 Jul 9	21	3	1392	F	C	
Carter	Emma		1931 Oct 19	1931 Oct 26	21	1	1602	F	C	
Carter	Emma		1934 Nov 15	1934 Nov 20	21	3	1374	F	C	
Carter	Frederick	C.								
Carter	James	E.	1933 Jun 13	1933 Jun 20	28	4	101A	M	C	
Carter	John		1927 Nov 11	1927 Nov 16	19	3	912		C	

LAST NAME	FIRST NAME	MIDDLE	DIED	INTERRED	SEC.	ROW	GRAVE	G	R	REMARKS
Carter	Jordan									
Carter	Josephine									
Carter	Katie									
Carter	Mary									
Carter	Nellie									
Carter	William	E.								
Cartey	James	O.	1918 Nov 21	1918 Nov 26	23	1	1657			(Cartey, William D.)
Cartey	William	D.								See: Cartey, James O.
Carthuser	Frank	K.	1934 Mar 27	1934 Apr 3	28	5	125A	M	W	
Cartwright	Leanna		1932 Jan 6	1932 Jan 12	21	1	1605	F	C	
Carum	Arnold		1932 Sep 30	1932 Oct 4	28	3	74A	M	C	
Cascio	Catherine	W.								
Cash	Charles									
Cash	Madeline		1935 Mar 6	1935 Mar 15	21	3	1386	F	C	
Casoligic	Lewis		1936 Jan 26	1936 Jan 29	29	3	228A	M	W	
Casson	Ella									
Casteel	Arnold									
Castleman	Wilfred									
Catherine	Lake									
Catton	Walter									
Caufield	Sarah									
Cays	Thomas		1919 Apr 29	1919 May 2	23	1	1683			
Chadwell	Margaret									
Chambers	Mattie		1934 Jan 14	1934 Jan 18	21	4	1498	F	C	
Champion	Thomas	L.								
Chaney	Ezekiel	F.								
Chaney	Mary		1936 Jun 10	1936 Jun 4	29	3	210A	F	C	
Chapetti	Cosomo		1929 May 17	1929 May 23	19	5	1108			
Chapman	Henry		1929 Dec 14	1929 Dec 19	19	5	1127			
Chapman	Mary									
Chapman	Nancy		1929 Mar 1	1929 Mar 7	20	4	1256			
Charles	Jack									
Charlie	George		1934 Mar 24	1934 Mar 30	28	5	126A	M	R	Indian Patient
Chart	Henry		1918 Apr 23	1918 Apr 26	13	4	152			
Chase	Maggie									
Cheatham	Lonnie									
Cheros	Clarence									
Cheshire	Louis	F.								

LAST NAME	FIRST NAME	MIDDLE	DIED	INTERRED	SEC.	ROW	GRAVE	G	R	REMARKS
Chester	Amanda	E.								
Chiera	John									
Childs	Bertha									
Chinn	Henry									
Chisholm	Corrine	D.								
Chong	Chien	C.								
Choppia	Alice		1935 Jul 15	1935 Jul 18	21	3	1394	F	C	
Christensen	Peder									
Christian	Marie									
Christiansen	Carl									
Chuponie	Tom									
Cittens	Catherine									Ashes
Clanton	Turner		1917 Oct 15	1917 Oct 18	22	3	1421	F		
Clark	Addie		1934 May 5	1934 May 9	21	4	1503	F	C	
Clark	Ann	Nancy								
Clark	Charles									See: Clark, William
Clark	Elizabeth									See: Ridgeley, George
Clark	George	D.								
Clark	George									
Clark	George		1919 Apr 21	1919 Apr 26	23	1	1682			
Clark	George									
Clark	Hanson									
Clark	Irene		1919 Sep 8	1919 Sep 11	20	1	1584			
Clark	James		1918 Jun 26	1918 Jun 28	18	4	979			
Clark	Joseph		1933 Dec 17	1933 Dec 21	28	5	138A	M	C	
Clark	Josephine									
Clark	Madeline									
Clark	Maude									
Clark	Minnie									
Clark	William		1934 Jan 20	1934 Jan 24	28	5	133A	M	W	
Clark	William									General Army Prisoner; (Clark, George D.)
Clatterbuck	James	E.								
Clay	Duster									See: Duster, Clay
Clay	Margaret		1937 Jan 31	1937 Feb 3	21	5	1167	F	C	
Clay	Philip		1926 Nov 4	1926 Nov 9	19	2	793			
Cleary	Mary									
Cleaves	Zaidu	F.	1929 Feb 26	1929 Mar 5	20	4	1255			
Clemens	Henry									
Clemens	Sherman									

LAST NAME	FIRST NAME	MIDDLE	DIED	INTERRED	SEC.	ROW	GRAVE	G	R	REMARKS
Clemmenson	Juliane									
Clomax	William	H.								
Clowden	Ferdinand									
Coates	David									
Coats	James	J.	1924 Dec 5	1924 Dec 9	23	5	1215			
Coats	Richard		1937 Aug 2	1937 Aug 5	29	5	283A	M	C	
Cohen	John									
Cole	Daniel		1927 Oct 2	1927 Oct 8	19	3	908			
Cole	Elizabeth		1925 Sep 7	1925 Sep 10	20	5	1476			
Cole	James	J.								
Cole	John	W.								
Coleman	James	A.								
Coles	Charles	A.								
Colfer	Michael									
Colgan	Fred		1917 Dec 21	1917 Dec 26	3	9	1585			
Collins	Cellie									See: Cowen, Grant
Collins	Grant									
Collins	Hannah	M.								
Collins	J.	Emma								
Collins	Mary	E.	1917 Aug 10	1917 Aug 14	25	5	1715			
Collins	Patrick									
Collins	Robert									
Colton	George									
Connally	John		1935 Jul 7	1935 Jul 8	29	2	186A	M	W	
Connell	William		1923 Jun 3	1923 Jun 8	23	4	1330			
Connelley	Thomas		1917 Jul 19	1917 Jul 21	3	9	1595			
Connelly	Albert	S.								
Connelly	Thomas									
Connelly	William	B								
Connor	Michael									
Conway	Charles		1920 Mar 29	1920 Apr 1	23	3	1429			
Conway	Julia		1926 Feb 5	1926 Feb 10	20	2	1479			
Conway	Margaret		1926 Mar 11	1926 Mar 17	20	3	1344			
Cook	Anderson		1934 Jan 6	1934 Jan 13	28	5	134A	M	C	
Cook	Franklin	T.	1927 Jul 2	1927 Jul 7	19	3	903			
Cooks	Luther	T.								
Coombs	Anna									
Coombs	Bernard	J.								
Coon	Charles		1932 Nov 14	1932 Nov 17	28	3	66A	M	C	

LAST NAME	FIRST NAME	MIDDLE	DIED	INTERRED	SEC.	ROW	GRAVE	G	R	REMARKS
Cooney	John	A.	1926 May 28	1926 Jun 4	19	1	689			
Cooper	Benjamin	E.								
Cooper	Edward	J.								
Cooper	Fred			1936 Dec 31	29	4	251A			
Cooper	Helen		1931 Feb 10	1931 Feb 14	20	5	1155	F	W	
Cooper	Lauretta		1929 Apr 24	1929 Apr 27	20	4	1261			
Cooper	Lillian	L.	1936 Jun 20	1936 Jun 25	29	3	209A	F	W	
Cooper	Ollie									
Coosenberry	Valentine		1927 Jan 24	1927 Jan 28	19	2	804			
Copeland	Sidney									
Coqueran	Eugena									
Corbin	John	M.								
Corbin	Mary		1936 Aug 27	1936 Aug 28	29	3	205	F	W	
Corcoran	Annie		1929 Mar 21	1929 Mar 26	20	4	1258			
Corcoran	Mary		1920 Mar 20	1920 Mar 23	20	1	1589			
Corlies	Marion									
Cornelius	Hanley									
Corrigan	Agnes									
Corturiendt	Sidney	F.								
Costa	Frank									
Coulterer	Irving									
Coupland	William									
Courtney	Cornelius		1928 Oct 25	1928 Oct 30	19	4	1012			
Courtney	Mary									
Cousins	J.	C.	1925 Feb 6	1925 Feb 10	23	5	1221			
Cowen	Grant		1919 Jan 31	1919 Feb 4	23	1	1669			Alias: Collins
Cowling	Leah	E. H.								
Cox	Bertha									
Craford	Jesse	J.								
Craig	Flavella		1927 Sep 15	1927 Sep 21	20	3	1363			
Craig	William		1937 Oct 19	1937 Oct 25	29	5	267A	M	C	
Crane	Alice	V.	1932 May 5	1932 May 12	21	5	1613	F	W	
Crawford	Anna									
Crawford	James									
Crawford	Norman	C.								
Crawford	Ruth									
Crawley	George									
Creacy	Mary									
Creed	Isaac									

LAST NAME	FIRST NAME	MIDDLE	DIED	INTERRED	SEC.	ROW	GRAVE	G	R	REMARKS
Creeping	Charles									Indian
Creigton	Jack		1928 Jan 11	1928 Jan 17	19	3	916			
Criselda	John									
Cronkhite	Belle									
Cross	Henry	W.								
Cross	Malinds									
Cross	Walter		1935 Dec 12	1935 Dec 17	29	3	231A	M	W	
Crostic	William									
Crowell	Harry	M.	1932 Aug 5	1932 Aug 12	28	3	78A	M	W	
Crowley	Emma									
Croy	Scott	H.								
Cruickshank	Robert									
Crunorto	Francisco		1935 Jan 29	1935 Feb 5	29	1	151A	M	W	
Cullen	William	R.								
Cummings	John									
Cunningham	Vincent									
Cunnings	John	M.								
Currans	Walter									
Curry	Edward									
Curtis	Joseph									
Curtis	Joseph									
Curtis	Josephine									
Curtis	Lottie									
Curtis	Lucy	O.								
Curtis	Roy									
Curto	Lazarus									
Dabney	William		1927 Feb 22	1927 Feb 26	19	2	810			
Dade	Randy									
Dahrooge	George		1931 Jul 3	1931 Jul 9	28	2	46A	M	W	
Daley	John	H.	1918 Jul 30	1918 Aug 2	22	4	1312			
Dalme	Louis		1933 Apr 6	1933 Apr 13	28	4	110A	M	C	
Dameron	Norton		1930 Apr 4	1930 Apr 8	28	1	22A			
D'Amico	John									
Damsey	Jack									
Danforth	Sherman									
Dangerfield	Daniel		1930 Sep 9	1930 Sep 16	28	1	6A	M	C	
Daniel	Antoinette									
Daniel	Delta									Virgin Islands
Daniels	Arthur		1928 Jan 24	1928 Jan 31	15	2	208			

LAST NAME	FIRST NAME	MIDDLE	DIED	INTERRED	SEC.	ROW	GRAVE	G	R	REMARKS
Daniels	George	D.								
Daniels	John									
Daniels	Lucille									
Daniels	Walter	B.	1929 Jul 23	1929 Jul 29	19	2	795			
Daniri	Areangelo									
Darrell	Walter									
Daucett	Thomas		1925 May 14	1925 May 18	23	5	1227			
Davidge	James		1928 Mar 9	1928 Mar 13	19	3	921			
Davidson	Harriet									
Davidson	Rehenia									
Davis	Addie	M.								
Davis	Annie	P.								
Davis	Cadwaler									
Davis	Charles	E.	1918 Dec 15	1918 Dec 19	23	1	1662			See: Doe, Mary
Davis	Della									
Davis	Doris	L.								
Davis	Edward									
Davis	George									See: Howell, George
Davis	George									
Davis	Helen									
Davis	James	E.	1918 Oct 26	1918 Oct 29	3	10	1779			
Davis	James									
Davis	Jesse									
Davis	Mable		1928 May 15	1928 May 21	20	4	1239			
Davis	Pearl									
Davis	Robert	L.								
Davis	Roy									
Davis	Samuel		1918 Dec 5	1918 Dec 9	23	1	1659			
Davis	William									
Davison	Edith		1919 Jul 31	1919 Aug 2	20	1	1581			
Dawling	May									
Dawson	Robert	J.								
Dawson	William									
Day	Laura		1918 Dec 27	1918 Dec 31	20	1	1570			
Dayton	Julia		1933 Nov 19	1933 Nov 23	21	4	1496	F	C	
Deabalo	Jacob									
Dean	Elizabeth									
DeFarges	Justin		1918 Feb 13	1918 Feb 15	22	4	1296			
Degrayter	Albert		1931 Jul 14	1931 Jul 17	28	2	44A	M	W	

LAST NAME	FIRST NAME	MIDDLE	DIED	INTERRED	SEC.	ROW	GRAVE	G	R	REMARKS
Delarne	Mary									D. C. Prisoner
Dello	Christos									
DeLoach	Carl									
DeLoss	Charles	L.								
Demont	John									See: Doe, John (Denehy)
Denchey	David		1917 Nov 3	1917 Nov 6	18	3	882			
Denehy	David									See: Denchey, Davis
Denham	Alfred	M.								
Denis	Roman		1926 Sep 22	1926 Sep 27	19	2	785			
Dennis	George	T.								
Dennison	William		1929 00 00	1929 May 9	19	5	1111			
Dephonso	Nick									
Derain	William									
Dermanious	James									
Dervisevich	Aliza		1927 Mar 30	1927 Apr 2	19	2	812			
DeSouza	Thomas		1926 Jun 16	1926 Jun 22	19	1	693			
Despar	William	H.								
Despaton	Theoriton									
Dessure	Carlin									
Detmering	Aaron									
DeVan	Lizzie									
Dewey	Elizabeth									
Dewey	Irving	W.								
Dias	John									
DiCarle	Recco									
Dick	Edward		1926 Mar 12	1926 Mar 23	19	1	679			
Diggs	James									
Diggs	Thomas	L.								
Diles	Alice									
Dillon	Cornelius									
Dixon	Alice									
Dixon	Elmer	R.								
Dixon	Richard		1936 Nov 4	1936 Oct 28	29	4	256A	M	C	[Death and burial dates possibly reversed.]
Dockery	Stanton									See: Dockety, Thornton (Stanton)
Dockery	Thornton									Alias: Demont
Doe	John		1917 Oct 12	1917 Oct 15	18	3	880			
Doe	John		1918 Oct 22	1918 Oct 23	22	5	1199			
Doe	John		1919 Apr 5	1919 Apr 8	23	1	1679			
Doe	John									A.K.A.: Britts, Joseph E.

LAST NAME	FIRST NAME	MIDDLE	DIED	INTERRED	SEC.	ROW	GRAVE	G	R	REMARKS
Doe	John (11th)									
Doe	Mary									(Della Davis)
Dolan	James									
Donaghue	Leo	J.								
Donahue	George	A.								
Donald	Lee		1924 Dec 13	1924 Dec 17	23	4	1216			
Donigan	Hugh	E.								
Donnelly	Hugh		1926 Apr 7	1926 Apr 14	19	1	685			
Donnelly	Michael									
Donoghue	William									
Donohoe	John		1936 Sep 25	1936 Sep 17	29	4	260A	M	W	[Death and burial dates possibly reversed.]
Donovan	Ambrose									
Dorsett	Nona									
Dorsey	Albert		1924 Jun 28	1924 Jul 2	23	5	1209			
Dorsey	Alberta									
Dorsey	Benjamin									
Dorsey	Charles	H.								
Dorsey	Fannie	M.								
Dorsey	George	A.								
Dorsey	Peter	M.								
Dorsey	Sophronia									
Dotts	Catherine									
Doubler	Abraham	L.	1918 Oct 23	1918 Oct 25	18	4	993			
Douf	Hattie	A.								
Dougherty	Mabel									
Douglas	Frank		1927 Aug 17	1927 Aug 20	19	3	905			
Douglas	Henry		1937 Feb 5	1937 Feb 11	29	4	244A	M	W	
Douglas	James		1933 Jun 26	1933 Jul 3	28	4	99A	M	C	
Douglas	Mary									
Douglas	James									
Douma	Herman									
Dovcakes	John	C.								
Dove	Bessie									
Dowling	Agnes									
Downs	Wilver									
Dowsey	Frank		1934 May 22	1934 May 29	29	1	174A	M	C	
Doyle	Frances									
Doyle	William	J.	1935 Apr 12	1935 Apr 18	29	2	198A	M	W	
Dozier	Robert									

LAST NAME	FIRST NAME	MIDDLE	DIED	INTERRED	SEC.	ROW	GRAVE	G	R	REMARKS
Drake	Mamie									
Dreas	Gus	A.	1937 Nov 13	1937 Nov 19	29	5	266A	M	W	
Dreher	Carl	F.								
Drew	Lucy									
Dreyer	Mollie									See: Dryer, Mary
Driggers	Peggy									
Driscoll	Charles	J.	1925 Nov 29	1925 Dec 3	15	1	112			
Dryer	Mary									Mollie Dreyer
DuBois	Jacques									
Duckett	John									
Duckett	Joseph									
Duckett	Sylvester		1921 Mar 9	1921 Mar 12	23	3	1437			
Duckett	Willard									
Dudas	Mary									
Dudley	Rose									
Dugistino	Guy		1928 May 3	1928 May 8	19	4	1003			
Duke	Petter	M.								
Dumas	Charlas	W.								
Dunbar	Henry									
Duncon	Eliza									
Dunn	Patrick	J.								
Durant	Francisco	S.	1927 Sep 28	1927 Oct 4	19	3	907			
Durasoff	S.	Nina								
Durham	Mary									
Durig	Ernest									
Duster	Clay		1921 Dec 2	1921 Dec 6	23	3	1446			Or: Clay, Duster
Dvis	Ernest									
Dwyer	John									
Dyer	Eliza									
Dyer	Frank		1918 Nov 16	1918 Nov 19	22	5	1207			
Dyer	Howard									
Dyer	Mabel									
Dyer	Margaret									
Dyson	Peter		1933 Feb 15	1933 Feb 21	28	3	59A	M	C	
Dyson	Sarah									
Earley	Elwood	J.	1935 Oct 7	1935 Oct 12	29	2	174A	M	C	
Easterling	Edith									
Eastman	Gustave									
Eberhart	Roscoe		1926 Jul 10	1926 Jul 15	19	1	696			

LAST NAME	FIRST NAME	MIDDLE	DIED	INTERRED	SEC.	ROW	GRAVE	G	R	REMARKS
Eckert	Emma									
Eckert	Otto		1937 Nov 5	1937 Nov 10	29	5	263A	M	W	
Edward	Augusta	R.								
Edwards	Bertha	M.								
Edwards	Inez									
Edwards	Lee	F.								
Edwards	Raymond		1930 Mar 9	1930 Mar 15	28	1	25A			
Ehlers	Frederick									
Ehlers	John		1937 Feb 7	1937 Feb 11	29	4	243A	M	W	
Ehman	Fritz									
Ehrman	Laurice									
Eibner	Fred		1930 Feb 22	1930 Mar 1	28	1	28A			
Eick	Fred		1919 May 2	1919 May 5	23	1	1684			
Eidler	Rosa									See: Briggs, Rosa
Eleazier	Hargett									
Elias	George									
Elkins	Phillip									
Elliott	Francis									
Elliott	Isabelle									
Elliott	William		1918 Nov 15	1918 Nov 19	23	1	1656			
Ellis	Amy									
Ellis	Miner									
Ellis	Sarah									
Ellis	William		1926 Dec 8	1926 Dec 15	15	2	206			
Ellmaker	Horace		1924 Feb 10	1924 Feb 13	23	4	1340			
Ellwood	Louine	H.	1937 Dec 25	1937 Dec 30	21	5	1177	F	W	
Elo	Owa	Aucel	1935 Sep 18	1935 Sep 23	29	2	176A	M	W	
Emiel	John									See: Franklin, William
Eminisor	Pauline									
Emory	Mary	E.								
Ensign	Meda		1935 Oct 11	1935 Oct 17	21	4	1270			Indian
Epps	Fannie									
Epps	Martha	A.								
Epps	William	W.								
Epps	William									
Erickson	Oscar		1937 Sep 18	1937 Sep 22	29	5	274A	M	W	
Eruery	Chappell		1933 Apr 28	1933 May 3	28	4	107A	M	C	
Esmill	Cadyna									See: Esmrile, Cadyna
Esmrile	Cadyna		1918 Oct 20	1918 Oct 22	22	5	1195			(Esmill)

LAST NAME	FIRST NAME	MIDDLE	DIED	INTERRED	SEC.	ROW	GRAVE	G	R	REMARKS
Eugman	Nils		1928 Jan 20	1928 Jan 26	19	4	1021			
Eullmer	Agnes	T.								
Eurico	Merii									
Evans	Augusta									
Evans	Frank									
Evans	Gertrude									
Evans	Harry	J.	1935 Aug 8	1935 Aug 13	29	2	181A	M	W	
Evans	Hazel									
Evans	Marie									
Everett	Hattie									
Everett	Lee									
Everhart	Margie									
Evry	George									
Failma	Felipe	A.								
Fairbanks	Ella	V.	1929 Mar 21	1929 Mar 27	20	4	1259			
Fairbanks	Richard		1935 Mar 10	1935 Mar 15	29	1	146A	M	I	Indian
Fairfax	Florence		1937 May 25	1937 Jun 2	21	5	1171	F	W	
Fairfield	Herrick		1934 Feb 12	1934 Feb 15	28	5	130A	M	W	
Falls	Effie									
Faltermayer	Adam									
Fandel	Emerick									
Fappiono	Joseph	G.								
Farmer	Rose									
Farnon	James		1921 Aug 15	1921 Aug 18	15	1	100			(Farnon)
Farnon	James									See: Farnnon, James
Farnsworth	Zane	J.								
Farr	Frank									
Farrell	Earl									
Faukner	Thomas		1937 Oct 12	1937 Oct 18	29	5	269A	M	C	
Fauntleroy	William									
Fearting	Mary									Disinterred Aug. 23, 1924
Fellerbauer	Stephen		1937 Mar 3	1937 Mar 8	29	4	240A	M	W	
Fellows	Jane	E.								
Fender	Thelma									
Fenstermaker	Christian									See: Fundemaker, Christian
Feole	John									
Ferguson	Elizabeth									
Fern	Frank									
Ferntakes	George									

LAST NAME	FIRST NAME	MIDDLE	DIED	INTERRED	SEC.	ROW	GRAVE	G	R	REMARKS
Ferrell	William									
Ferri	Leopold		1931 Sep 18	1931 Oct 22	28	2	38A			Alias: Von Ferri
Ferry	Charles	E.								
Ficken	Henry	W.								
Fields	Joseph									
Filiz	Pascual		1933 Dec 10	1933 Dec 16	28	5	139A	M	W	
Finn	Austin									
Finsley	Robert									
Fisher	Benjamin	W.								
Fishtrap	James									
Fitzgerald	Anne									
Fitzhugh	George	W.								
Fitzwater	Byrne		1919 Jan 3	1919 Jan 7	18	5	1085			
Flavin	John		1937 Apr 28	1937 May 5	29	4	234A	M	W	
Fleet	John	E.	1935 Feb 23	1935 Feb 28	29	1	148A	M	C	
Fleet	Mary									
Flemming	Mary	A.	1927 Sep 22	1027 Sep 28	20	3	1364			
Fletcher	Harriett		1935 Aug 26	1935 Aug 30	21	3	1397	F	C	
Fletcher	Nona									
Fletcher	Willie									
Flood	George	W.								
Fods	Paul	C.	1934 May 20	1934 May 24	28	5	117A	M	W	
Foley	Maurice		1936 Nov 24	1936 Nov 19	21	5	1164	M	W	[Death and burial dates possibly reversed.]
Foley	Thomas		1918 Feb 28	1918 Mar 4	18	3	889			
Folivan	Henry		1918 Oct 5	1918 Oct 8	22	5	1190			
Fondell	William									
Ford	Florence									
Ford	John		1932 Feb 3	1932 Feb 10	28	2	35A	M	W	
Ford	Urias									
Forrest	Annie		1928 Apr 7	1928 Apr 10	20	4	1238			
Forrest	Lillian									
Forrest	Raymond	M.								
Forrester	Alice		1925 Jan 31	1925 Feb 9	20	2	1469			
Forsyth	Edith									
Fortes	Jack									
Fortney	Gertrode		1920 Dec 6	1920 Dec 7	20	1	1596			
Foster	Bessie		1935 Jun 7	1935 Jun 12	21	3	1390	F	W	
Foster	Carrie									
Foster	Nettie	J.								

LAST NAME	FIRST NAME	MIDDLE	DIED	INTERRED	SEC.	ROW	GRAVE	G	R	REMARKS
Foster	Philip									
Foster	Rosie		1931 May 1	1931 May 7	20	5	1159		C	
Foster	Roy									
Foster	Vernon	A.	1926 Nov 12	1926 Nov 17	19	2	795			Disinterred July 5, 1929
Fountaine	Joe	L.								
Fowler	Jacob	L.								
Fowler	Jane									
Fowler	Lottie		1919 Jan 19	1919 Jan 22	20	1	1576			
Fowler	Mabel	H.								
Fox	Fannie		1928 Sep 25	1928 Oct 1	20	4	1246			
Fox	Michael									
Fox	William		1924 May 28	1924 Jun 2	23	4	1342			
Foy	Daniel									
Foy	James		1933 Aug 8	1933 Aug 22	28	4	91A	M	W	
Fragonine	Frank		1918 Aug 7	1918 Aug 12	22	5	1185			
Frambrough	Zevonia	L.								Alias: Emiel, John
Franklin	William		1927 May 17	1927 May 24	19	3	901			
Freeher	Annie									
Freeher	Emmett									
Freeman	Annie	B.								
Freeman	Landonia									
French	Joseph									
Freschkned	Edward		1937 Feb 3	1937 Feb 9	29	4	246A	M	W	Exhumed June 21, 1937.
Fresnedi	John									
Fretzer	James	A.								
Frido	William		1925 Feb 14	1925 Feb 17	23	5	1222			
Frisoni	Frank									
Fritzsche	Edward									
Frobey	Agnes		1929 Oct 28	1929 Nov 4	20	5	1133			
Frowner	Emma		1935 Aug 13	1935 Aug 15	21	3	1396	F	W	
Frye	Ceatta									
Frye	Douglas	A.								
Frye	Emma									
Frye	Lucy									
Fulford	William	H.	1932 Apr 26	1932 May 2	28	3	84A	M	C	
Fuller	John									
Fulton	Callie									
Fundemaker	Christian		1929 Feb 13	1929 Feb 18	19	4	1024			Alias: Fenstermaker
Fundulakis	Emanuel		1925 Feb 1	1925 Feb 4	15	1	111			

LAST NAME	FIRST NAME	MIDDLE	DIED	INTERRED	SEC.	ROW	GRAVE	G	R	REMARKS
Furguson	Daniel									
Gaboy	Arthur									
Gabriel	Ferdinand									
Gaines	Belle									
Gaines	Emma		1931 May 4	1931 May 13	20	5	1160	F	C	
Gaines	Matilda	V.								
Gaither	Eliza									
Galem	Paul	A.								
Gallagher	Rosie		1933 Jan 3	1933 Jan 9	21	5	1625	F	W	
Gallaher	John									
Gallion	Elmer	S.	1917 Dec 10	1917 Dec 13	18	3	884			
Gander	Frank									
Gant	Joe									
Ganus	Joseph		1937 Oct 29	1937 Nov 2	29	5	264A	M	W	
Garcad	Christine		1926 May 2	1926 May 6	20	3	1348			(Christiana)
Gardner	Listerene									
Gardner	Lucy	M.								
Gardner	Oliver		1926 Apr 1	1926 Apr 6	20	3	1346			
Garner	Josephine	N.	1936 Feb 5	1936 Feb 10	21	4	1278	F	C	
Garnett	Jerry									
Garten	Gertrude	W.								
Garten	John		1919 Sep 1	1919 Sep 4	15	1	91			
Garton	Louise									
Garwood	Wilberforce		1919 Apr 20	919 Apr 23	18	5	1096			
Gaskins	Alfred	J.								
Gaskins	Eugene									
Gaskins	Lula									
Gassaway	Malinda		1935 Mar 2	1935 Mar 9	21	3	1385	F	C	
Gates	James		1922 Dec 2	1922 Dec 5	23	4	1321			
Gathright	Lonni									
Gatto	Antonio									
Gatton	James		1919 Feb 20	1919 Feb 25	23	1	1672			
Gaufney	James									
Gay	Melvin									
Gayle	Catherine	H.								
Geaney	Catherine									
Geary	John		1918 Nov 17	1918 Nov 21	18	5	1081			
Geary	Samuel		1930 Mar 4	1930 Mar 10	28	1	27A			
Gedney	Linda	B.								

LAST NAME	FIRST NAME	MIDDLE	DIED	INTERRED	SEC.	ROW	GRAVE	G	R	REMARKS
Geiman	Bernice									
Gemmett	Louis									
Gentry	Jenny		1933 Jun 2	1933 Jun 6	21	4	1486	F	C	
George	Georgiana		1917 Oct 13	1917 Oct 17	25	5	1720			(Johanna)
George	Johanna									See: George, Georgianna
George	Lloyd									
George	Mable									
Gerard	Emile									
Gerguson	Carrie									
Gerriti	Ignatzio									
Gespeda	Guillermo									
Geyer	Harold		1933 Jun 24	1933 Jun 28	28	4	100A	M	W	
Gibbins	Patrick		1937 Jan 20	1937 Jan 26	15	2	213	M	W	
Gibson	Edward		1930 Nov 13	1930 Nov 18	28	1	2A	M	C	
Gibson	Elizabeth									
Gibson	Joseph									
Gibson	Peter									
Gibson	Raymond									
Gibson	Robert									
Gibson	William									
Gilbert	Charles									
Gilbert	Randolph									
Gill	Albert	E.								
Gill	Nellie		1936 Apr 8	1936 Apr 15	1	4	1285	F	W	
Gillam	Wesley		1927 Feb 24	1927 Mar 1	19	2	811			
Gillenwater	Frank		1931 Jul 30	1931 Aug 5	28	2	43A	M	W	
Gillespie	Richard		1926 Oct 19	1926 Oc 26	15	2	205			
Gingell	Johanna	P.	1928 Aug 27	1928 Sep 1	20	4	1244			
Ginty	Frank	J.								
Gladys	Hazel									
Glancy	Effie	L.								
Glenn	John	C.								
Glore	Arthur	M.	1929 Sep 15	1929 Sep 19	19	5	1121			U.S.P.
Glover	John									
Glover	Mary		1934 Jul 25	1934 Aug 1	21	4	1507	F	C	
Golbertine	Gus		1926 Apr 4	1926 Apr 8	19	1	683			(Golbertin)
Goldstein	Fred	D.								
Gonzalez	Pablo	B.								
Goode	Ella									

LAST NAME	FIRST NAME	MIDDLE	DIED	INTERRED	SEC.	ROW	GRAVE	G	R	REMARKS
Goode	L.	Rosa								
Goodman	Frank									
Goodman	Henry	T.								
Gordon	Eugenie		1935 Jul 11	1935 Jul 16	21	3	1393	F	W	Still birth.
Gordon	Jean									
Gordon	Mary									Virgin Islands
Gordon	William		1930 Mar 5	1930 Mar 12	28	1	26A			
Gorman	Denham		1920 Feb 13	1920 Feb 16	23	3	1427			
Gould	Felix		1926 Oct 14	1926 Oct 20	19	2	791			
Gow	John	E.	1934 Sep 25	1934 Oct 2	29	1	164A	M	W	
Grady	Earle	G.								
Grady	Marion	J.								
Graham	Mattie									
Graham	Robert		1923 Feb 5	1923 Feb 8	23	4	1324			
Grandison	Charles									
Grandison	Mary	W.								
Grant	Charles									
Grant	Fred	A.								
Grant	James									
Grant	Joseph									
Grant	Richard		1932 Aug 23	1932 Aug 29	28	3	76A	M	W	
Grash	Emory		1933 Apr 7	1933 Apr 11	28	4	111A	M	W	
Graves	Alice									
Graves	Harold		1929 Oct 20	1929 Oct 29	18	5	1123			Alias: Hunter
Graves	Samuel	S.								
Graves	Thomas	E.	1937 Aug 4	1937 Aug 9	29	5	282A	M	W	
Gray	Benjamin									
Gray	Edward	E.	1926 Feb 28	1926 Mar 5	24	1	2169			Body was claimed.
Gray	Hattie									
Gray	Homer									
Gray	James									
Gray	Jean									
Gray	JoAnn									
Gray	John		1928 Jan 14	1928 Jan 14	19	4	1019			
Gray	Leo		1932 Apr 10	1932 Apr 13	28	3	85A	M	C	
Gray	Mary									
Grayson	Dauid		1932 Oct 29	1932 Nov 5	28	3	69A	F	C	
Grayson	Hattie		1935 Nov 14	1935 Nov 18	21	4	1272	F	C	
Grayson	Viola	V.								

LAST NAME	FIRST NAME	MIDDLE	DIED	INTERRED	SEC.	ROW	GRAVE	G	R	REMARKS
Green	Alice		1923 Oct 15	1923 Oct 20	20	2	1464		C	
Green	Anna		1931 Mar 3	1931 Mar 10	20	5	1157	F		
Green	Belle		1929 Jan 6	1929 Feb 12	20	4	1251			
Green	Edward	R.								
Green	Elizebeth		1928 Dec 10	1928 Dec 15	20	4	1248			
Green	Ethel									
Green	Gertrude									
Green	Heily									See: Green, Henry
Green	Henry		1931 Jul 10	1931 Jul 17	28	2	45A	M	W	Alias: Heily
Green	Herman	T.	1933 May 23	1933 May 29	28	4	104	M	C	
Green	James	O.								
Green	James									
Green	Janie									
Green	John									
Green	Mary	E.	1936 Mar 11	1936 Mar 17	21	4	1282	F	C	
Green	Minnie	E.								
Green	Ralf		1930 Mar 10	1930 Mar 17	28	1	24A			
Green	Richard		1934 Sep 1	1934 Sep 6	29	1	166A	M	C	
Green	Walter									
Green	William		1929 Mar 15	1929 Mar 20	19	5	1105			
Green	William									
Green	William									
Greenley	Griffin									
Greenly	Mary	M.	1936 Mar 31	1936 Apr 6	21	4	1284	F	W	
Greenwell	Emma		1932 Nov 26	1932 Nov 30	21	5	1623	F	C	
Greenwood	Arthur									
Greer	Mary		1934 Jan 29	1934 Feb 3	21	4	1499	F	W	
Gregory	George	A.								
Greley	James		1918 Oct 24	1918 Oct 26	18	4	995			
Grell	Joseph									(Grell, Joseph)
Grien	Thad	S.								See: Greley, James
Griffin	Argo	B.								
Griffin	Roosevelt									
Griffin	Sadie									
Griffith	Anna									
Griffith	Margaret									
Griswald	A.	Mary	1937 Mar 10	1937 Mar 15	21	5	1170	F	W	Exhumed December 3, 1941.
Grokom	Charles									
Grubbs	Alice	L.								

LAST NAME	FIRST NAME	MIDDLE	DIED	INTERRED	SEC.	ROW	GRAVE	G	R	REMARKS
Guidat	Julius									
Gutal	Wazil									
Haas	Kathleen									
Hackley	Lena		1931 Feb 3	1931 Feb 10	20	5	1154	F	C	
Hager	Nicholas		1928 Dec 1	1928 Dec 6	19	4	1017			
Hahn	Carl									
Halburtoa	Iasah		1918 Jun 13	1918 Jun 17	18	4	977			
Hall	Bertha									
Hall	Eliza		1932 May 1	1932 May 7	21	5	1612	F	C	
Hall	Elizabeth									
Hall	James									
Hall	John		1937 Jul 19	1937 Jul 23	29	5	285A	M	C	
Hall	Josephine									
Hall	William									
Haller	Desiderio									
Hamill	Cecile									
Hamilton	Benjamin	F.	1937 Mar 31	1937 Apr 5	29	4	236A	M	W	
Hamilton	William		1933 Apr 9	1933 Apr 24	28	4	109A	M	C	
Hampton	Curtis									
Hampton	Inez	N.								
Hand	Patrick									
Hands	Kate		1934 May 20	1934 May 24	21	4	1505	F	C	
Hangton	Janet									
Hanley	Cornelius									Disinterred Jul. 19, 1926 See: Cornelius, Hanley
Hannon	Ella									
Hansen	Felix									
Hansen	Vera									
Hanson	Charles		1918 Apr 10	1918 Apr 15	22	4	1303			
Hanson	Columbus									See: Harrison, Columbus
Hanson	Holbert									Virgin Islands
Hanson	John	P.								
Harakas	James	G.	1930 Jun 2	1930 Jun 9	28	1	17A			
Harbour	Curtis									
Harding	Jeremiah									
Hardman	Minnie									
Hardy	John	L.								
Hardy	Sadie									
Hargrave	Martha		1918 Nov 21	1918 Nov 25	25	5	1741			
Hargrove	Flora									

LAST NAME	FIRST NAME	MIDDLE	DIED	INTERRED	SEC.	ROW	GRAVE	G	R	REMARKS
Hargrove	Ruth									
Haring	Augustus	A.	1918 Oct 6	1918 Oct 10	22	5	1191			
Harkness	Kate		1932 Mar 19	1932 Mar 25	21	2	1610	F	W	
Harlee	John	W.	1930 Nov 24	1930 Dec 1	28	2	57A	M	W	
Harley	Lillian									
Harlow	Ida	L.								
Harlow	Robert	M.								
Harmon	Nettie	L.	1931 May 14	1931 May 19	20	5	1161	F	W	
Harmon	Theodore	C.								
Harp	Albert		1937 Mar 25	1937 Mar 30	29	4	238A	M	C	
Harper	Awry		1932 Aug 23	1932 Aug 30	28	3	75A	M	W	
Harriott	George		1926 Jun 10	1926 Jun 15	19	1	691			
Harris	Ann		1919 Jan 8	1919 Jan 13	20	1	1573			
Harris	Archie									
Harris	Blanche									
Harris	Eliza									
Harris	Elnora									
Harris	Estelle									
Harris	George		1934 Apr 10	1934 Apr 13	28	5	120A	M	C	
Harris	Margaret	A.								
Harris	Marion									
Harris	Susan		1934 Jun 8	1934 Jun 14	21	4	1506	F	C	
Harrison	Columbus		1931 Nov 16	1931 Nov 19	28	2	36A	M	C	Alias: Hanson
Hart	alberta									
Hart	George	R.	1935 Jan 17	1935 Jan 22	29	1	154A	M	C	
Hart	John	G.								
Harwood	Edwin		1923 Mar 20	1923 Mar 27	23	4	1328			
Haskins	James		1918 Dec 7	1918 Dec 12	23	1	1660			(Hawkins)
Haskins	John									
Haskins	Marshall		1921 Mar 5	1921 Mar 9	23	4	1314			
Hasky	Benjamin									
Hastings	Percy									
Hatch	Isadora									
Hatevick	Victor	C.	1937 Oct 15	1937 Oct 20	29	5	268A	M	W	
Hatton	Kathryn	A. S.								
Havenda	Victoria									
Hawkins	Alice									
Hawkins	James	S.								
Hawkins	James									See: Haskins, James

LAST NAME	FIRST NAME	MIDDLE	DIED	INTERRED	SEC.	ROW	GRAVE	G	R	REMARKS
Hawkins	James		1929 Aug 6	1919 Aug 13	19	5	1118			
Hawkins	Jennie		1929 Nov 1	1929 Nov 7	20	5	1134			
Hawkins	Mary									Disinterred Jun 18, 1926
Hawks	Maud	A.		1925 Jul 23	20	5	1475			
Hawley	Maud	T.								
Hayden	James		1936 May 12	1936 May 19	29	3	214A	M	C	
Haynes	Elisha									
Haynie	Harry	P.								
Haynie	James	S.								
Haywood	William	B.	1930 Jul 8	1930 Jul 15	28	1	13A	M	W	
Heckler	August									
Heflin	Grace									
Heido	August	S.	1933 Aug 1	1933 Aug 7	28	4	92A	M	W	U. S. Army Prisoner
Heiss	Lena	P.								
Heller	Matilda									
Henderson	Isiah	N.								
Henderson	Lee		1937 Feb 3	1937 Feb 8	29	4	247A	M	C	
Henderson	William									
Hendricks	Ferdinand									
Hendricks	James									
Henery	Imon									
Henley	Florence									
Hennessy	Herman									
Hennuray	Charles	F.								
Henry	joseph									
Henry	Louise									
Henry	William		1935 Jun 19	1935 Jun 24	29	2	188A	M	W	
Hensley	Elijah		1934 Jun 27	1934 Jun 30	29	1	171A	M	W	
Henson	George		1937 Oct 5	1937 Oct 11	29	5	272A	M	C	
Henson	John									
Henson	Richard									
Henston	Peter		1933 Jul 1	1933 Jul 10	28	4	95A	M	W	Alias: Houston
Henton	Robert									
Herick	Paul									
Herkenroder	Eva									
Herman	Getz									
Herndez	Mary	B.								
Herndon	Milan									
Herrstrom	William	J.	1928 apr 12	1928 Apr 17	19	4	1002			

LAST NAME	FIRST NAME	MIDDLE	DIED	INTERRED	SEC.	ROW	GRAVE	G	R	REMARKS
Heylinger	Roseline									
Hicks	Cora		1927 Feb 6	1927 Feb 12	20	3	1356			
Hicks	Preston									
Higgins	William									
Higgs	Charles	H.	1932 Mar 13	1932 Mar 17	28	2	30A	M	W	
Hilian	Carl		1937 Jun 18	1937 Jun 22	29	5	287A	M	W	
Hill	John	M.								
Hill	Richard									
Hill	William									
Hillard	Willie	M.								
Hilgrine	Alexander		1918 Jan 7	1918 Jan 9	22	4	1292			
Hilton	Garfield									
Hilton	Thomas	P.	1934 Apr 3	1934 Apr 10	28	5	121A	M	W	
Hinton	Marie									
Hirshburg	John									
Hixon	Virginia	W.	1928 Aug 18	1928 Aug 21	20	4	1241			
Hjabmer										See: James, Hjabmer
Hobbs	Marion		1917 Oct 13	1917 Oct 15	25	5	1719			
Hodgeman	John	A.								
Hoerrick	Augustus		1922 Jan 31	1922 Feb 7	20	2	1458			
Hoffman	Edward									
Hoffman	Victor		1928 Jul 5	1928 Jul 10	19	4	1006			
Hogan	Joseph	H.	1929 Oct 17	1929 Oct 17	19	5	1122			
Hogan	Wade									
Hoge	Sarah	R.								
Hohrein	Martin	W.	1925 Jun 3	1925 Jun 9	3	10	1749			
Hoke	James	F.	1925 Jul 14	1925 Jul 17	23	5	1232			(Wittey)
Holcomb	Mary									
Holden	Richard		1932 Oct 3	1932 Oct 6	28	3	73A	M	C	
Holland	Maria		1931 Oct 18	1931 Oct 23	21	1	1601	F	C	
Hollenzollern	Donna		1937 Mar 1	1937 Mar 4	21	5	1169	F	W	
Holliday	Allen		1937 Jan 00	1937 Jan 6	29	4	250A	M	C	
Hollway	Sebron									
Holman	Elizabeth									
Holmes	Lettie		1932 Mar 11	1932 Mar 16	21	1	1609	F	C	
Holom	John									
Holsey	Madison									
Holtz	Claw	Austin								
Holtzman	Aldred		1917 Oct 3	1917 Oct 5	22	3	1419			

LAST NAME	FIRST NAME	MIDDLE	DIED	INTERRED	SEC.	ROW	GRAVE	G	R	REMARKS
Hood	John	I.								
Hood	Julia									
Hopkins	Charles	J.								
Hopkins	Massie	J.								
Hoppney	William	Q.	1918 Apr 9	1918 Apr 12	22	4	1302			
Horton	Alfred		1936 Feb 1	1936 Feb 5	29	3	227A	M	W	Exhumed February 8, 1936.
Horton	Emma			1914 Mar 30	14	5	545			
Hose	Manuel		1917 Sep 9	1917 Sep 11	22	3	1416			
Hoskins	Major		1922 Mar 5	1922 Mar 11	23	3	1449			
Hotchkiss	Caroline									
Houston	Peter									See: Henston, Peter
Howard	Abraham									
Howard	Audrey									
Howard	Jennie		1934 Oct 6	1934 Oct 13	21	3	1373	F	C	
Howard	John		1933 Jul 1	1933 Jul 8	28	4	96A	M	C	
Howard	Mary									
Howard	Mattie									
Howard	William		1919 Jul 15	1919 Jul 17	23	2	1545			
Howell	George		1917 Dec 23	1917 Dec 27	18	3	886			
Hoyt	Gertrude		1917 Oct 2	1917 Oct 3	25	5	1717			Alias: Davis (Hoyte)
Hoyte	Gertrude									See: Hoyt, Gertrude
Hudson	Charles		1923 Feb 8	1923 Feb 12	23	4	1325			
Hudson	John	C.								
Hudson	William		1917 Aug 2	1917 Aug 6	18	3	876			
Hudson	William		1934 Feb 21	1934 Mar 1	28	5	138A	M	C	
Hudson	William									
Huges	Edith									
Hughes	Annia									
Hughes	Augustus		1932 Nov 7	1932 Nov 12	28	3	67A	M	W	
Hughes	Lucy	I.								
Hulse	William		1918 Oct 20	1918 Oct 22	18	4	989			
Hunber	James	L.								
Hunt	Berkley		1928 Jul 8	1928 Jul 12	19	4	1007			
Hunter	Harold		1929 Nov 29	1929 Dec 5	19	5	1126			
Hunter	James									See: Graves, Hunter
Hunter	John	H.								
Hunter	Philip									
Huntington	Arthur	W.	1937 Jul 11	1937 Jul 19	29	5	286A	M	W	
Huntsberry	George									

LAST NAME	FIRST NAME	MIDDLE	DIED	INTERRED	SEC.	ROW	GRAVE	G	R	REMARKS
Hurley	Albert									
Hutchings	John									See: John, Hutchings
Hutchins	William									
Hutchinson	E.	Francis								
Hutchinson	Geneva									
Hutzler	George		1918 Aug 18	1918 Aug 22	18	4	985			
Hyde	Leo	Milo								Disinterred Feb 5, 1924
Hydie	Mary									
Hynson	Archie									
Ida	Scott									
Iles	Robert									
Illegible	Anna	D. F.								[Death and burial dates possibly reversed.]
Ingwrsin	Lionel		1936 Dec13	1936 Dec 2	29	4	253A			
Innis	Robert									
Irby	William									
Isaiah	Luis									U. S. Army Prisoner
Ivry	Amela									
Jackson	Annie	M.								
Jackson	Annie									
Jackson	Annie									
Jackson	Annie									
Jackson	Charles		1936 Jan 12	1936 Jan 17	28	3	230A	M	C	
Jackson	Charlie									
Jackson	Charlotte	P.								
Jackson	Edward									
Jackson	Georgiana									Thomas, Jane
Jackson	Hatie		1919 Jul 20	1919 Jul 24	20	1	1578			
Jackson	Henry		1921 Mar 13	1921 Mar 15	23	4	1315			
Jackson	Henry									
Jackson	James	H.								
Jackson	Jerrell									
Jackson	John	E.								
Jackson	Laura									
Jackson	Lee		1929 Jun 20	1929 Jun 26	19	5	1112			
Jackson	Luther									
Jackson	Margaret		1933 Mar 2	1933 Mar 8	21	4	1482	F	C	
Jackson	Martha		1918 Apr 20	1918 Apr 24	25	5	1730			
Jackson	Martha									

LAST NAME	FIRST NAME	MIDDLE	DIED	INTERRED	SEC.	ROW	GRAVE	G	R	REMARKS
Jackson	Mary		1934 Feb 11	1934 Feb 17	21	4	1501	F	C	
Jackson	Mary									
Jackson	Missouri									Indian
Jackson	Pearl									
Jackson	Robert									
Jackson	Rose									
Jackson	Ruth									
Jackson	Stanley									
Jackson	William		1928 Mar 25	1928 Mar 31	19	4	1001			
Jackson	William		1931 Jun 11	1931 Jun 16	28	2	49A	M	C	
Jacobson	Petter		1930 Aug 25	1930 Sep 2	28	1	8A	M	W	
James	Arabelle									
James	Frank	C.								
James	Hjabmer									
James	Jessie									
James	John									
James	Louisa									
James	Robert									
James	Walter	S.	1919 Mar 26	1919 Mar 31	18	5	1095			
Jamison	Janie									
Janson	Gaston	M.								
Jararo	Dionacio									
Jarber	Lillian	R.	1919 Aug 6	1919 Aug 8	20	1	1582			
Jaskson	Eva		1918 May 5	1918 May 6	25	5	1732			
Javier	Ambrosio									
Jeanmeret	Anna	L.								
Jefferson	Charles		1920 Jun 23	1920 Jun 26	23	2	1558			
Jefferson	Dorothy		1929 Mar 11	1929 Mar 18	20	4	1257			
Jefferson	Ella		1932 Oct 3	1932 Oct 10	21	5	1621	F	C	
Jefferson	Frank		1934 Jul 3	1934 Jul 10	29	1	169A	M	C	
Jefferson	James		1930 Sep 30	1930 Oct 7	28	1	4A	M	C	
Jefferson	Nathaniel									
Jefferson	Susie									
Jefferson	Thomas		1937 Feb 1	1937 Feb 4	29	4	248A	M	C	
Jefferson	William									
Jenkins	Bud									
Jenkins	Cara									
Jenkins	Carrie		1928 Jan 1	1928 Jan 7	20	4	1249			
Jenkins	Delma	A.								

LAST NAME	FIRST NAME	MIDDLE	DIED	INTERRED	SEC.	ROW	GRAVE	G	R	REMARKS
Jenkins	George									
Jenkins	Tom									
Jenkins	William	Powell	1932 Feb 27	1932 Mar 3	22	1	Between	M	W	Bet. 1195 & 96; Inf. son of Delma A. Jenkins.
Jenkins	William									
Jennins	Agnes	B.								
Jessinghouse	Earnest									
Jeverson	Beverly		1930 May 11	1930 Jun 19	28	1	15A			
Jimmerson	Alice									
Jimmerson	Richard									
Johannsen	Johnnes									
John	Hutchings									
Johnsen	Rudolph									
Johnson	Affie									
Johnson	Albert	T.								
Johnson	Alford									
Johnson	Andrew	M.	1936 Feb 3	1936 Feb 10	29	3	227A	M	C	
Johnson	Anna									
Johnson	Annie									
Johnson	Annie									
Johnson	Arthur									
Johnson	Belle									
Johnson	Betty									
Johnson	Carl									
Johnson	Charles	C.								
Johnson	Charles		1935 Sep 23	1935 Sep 26	29	2	175A	M	C	
Johnson	Charles									
Johnson	Dorothy									
Johnson	Edmonia		1929 Feb 24	1929 Mar 2	20	4	1254			
Johnson	Elizabeeth									
Johnson	Emma									
Johnson	Fannie	B.								
Johnson	George	W.	1933 Feb 22	1933 Feb 28	28	4	114	M	C	
Johnson	George		1921 Aug 12	1921 Aug 16	23	3	1442			
Johnson	Granville									
Johnson	Harry									
Johnson	Hattis									
Johnson	Hazel	M.								
Johnson	Horton									
Johnson	Irving									

LAST NAME	FIRST NAME	MIDDLE	DIED	INTERRED	SEC.	ROW	GRAVE	G	R	REMARKS
Johnson	Isiah		1929 Jul 30	1929 Aug 1	19	5	1115			
Johnson	James									
Johnson	Joe		1928 Nov 12	1928 Nov 12	19	4	1014			
Johnson	John	M.								
Johnson	Josephine									
Johnson	Louis									
Johnson	Louise	R.								
Johnson	Ludwig									
Johnson	Martha									
Johnson	Mary	F.	1920 Sep 23	1920 Sep 27	20	1	1594			
Johnson	Mary		1937 Nov 28	1937 Dec 3	21	5	1176	F	C	
Johnson	Mildred									
Johnson	Oscar									
Johnson	P.	Grace								
Johnson	Richard									
Johnson	Rose		1918 Oct 3	1918 Oct 7	25	5	1740			
Johnson	Samuel									
Johnson	Sarah	L.								
Johnson	Thomas	O.	1918 Jul 2	1918 Jul 6	18	4	981			
Johnson	Thomas	S.								
Johnson	Warren									
Johnson	Wesley									
Johnson	Wiley									
Johnson	William	H.	1918 Jun 4	1918 Jun 6	22	4	1306			
Johnson	William									
Johnson	William									
Johnson	William									
Johnson	William									
Johnston	James	A.								
Joke	Joe									
Jolicoeur	Joseph									
Jones	Dell		1918 Jan 2	1918 Jan 4	22	4	1291			
Jones	Emma									
Jones	Frank									
Jones	Fred									
Jones	George									See: Taylor, George
Jones	George									
Jones	Helen									
Jones	Isabella	L.	1936 Jan 27	1936 Jan 30	21	4	1276	F	C	

LAST NAME	FIRST NAME	MIDDLE	DIED	INTERRED	SEC.	ROW	GRAVE	G	R	REMARKS
Jones	James	N.	1925 Jan 17	1925 Jan 22	15	1	110			
Jones	James									
Jones	James									
Jones	Jennie		1926 Nov 13	1926 Nov 18	20	3	1352			Alias: Svnelin, Clarence
Jones	John		1926 Feb 22	1926 Mar 1	19	1	674			
Jones	John		1927 Jan 31	1927 Feb 5	19	2	805			
Jones	Jordan		1932 Jun 11	1932 Jun 16	28	3	82A	M	C	
Jones	Julius									
Jones	Katie									
Jones	Mary	J.								
Jones	Phillip	A.								
Jones	Richard									
Jones	Sarah		1919 Jan 13	1919 Jan 15	20	1	1575			
Jones	Sarah									
Jones	Willie	M.								
Jones	Willie									
Jonesco	Zarva									
Jordan	Lawrence									
Jordan	Walter	J.								
Jordan	West, Jr.		1920 Oct 30	1920 Nov 3	23	2	1565			
Joseph	Marcy	Swasey								
Josephus	William		1933 Mar 25	1933 Mar 30	28	4	112A	M	C	
Joska	Steve		1926 Dec 2	1926 Dec 6	19	2	800			
Joyce	Martin		1919 Feb 26	1919 Feb 28	23	1	1673			
Joyce	Thomas									
Joyner	Charles	J.	1919 Apr 24	1919 Apr 28	18	5	1097			
Kagey	Branson									
Kaitola	Seymon									See: Kotzuba, Seymon
Kalitsis	Harry									
Kallis	Carrie									
Kalonuheskie	Edith		1937 Jan 6	1937 Jan 12	21	5	1165	F	I	Indian
Kaska	Charles									
Kavanagh	John	E.								
Kaykitt	Annette									
Keath	Jennie		1920 Mar 27	1920 Mar 29	20	1	1590			
Keating	Maurice		1928 Sep 15	1928 Sep 20	19	4	1009			
Keefer	Isaia									
Kehrli	Andrew		1926 Jun 25	1926 Jun 30	15	1	116			
Keilman	Herman		1920 Sep 12	1920 Sep 15	15	1	95			

LAST NAME	FIRST NAME	MIDDLE	DIED	INTERRED	SEC.	ROW	GRAVE	G	R	REMARKS
Keller	Emel		1918 Oct 19	1918 Oct 22	22	5	1196			
Keller	Frederick								W	
Kelley	Elizabeth		1931 Jan 17	1931 Jan 22	20	5	1152	F		
Kelley	Owen		1917 Nov 19	1917 Nov 22	22	3	1424			
Kelley	Pat		1925 Dec 12	1925 Dec 18	19	1	668			
Kelly	Edward		1934 Jan 6	1934 Jan 12	28	5	135A	M	C	
Kelly	James	A.								
Kelly	John	H.	1925 Feb 1	1925 Feb 4	23	5	1218			
Kelly	John									
Kelly	John									
Kelly	Michael									
Kelty	E.	William	1932 Dec 15	1932 Dec 20	28	3	64A	M	C	U. S. Army Prisoner
Kenney	Lena		1925 Mar 31	1925 Apr 6	20	2	1473			
Kent	Anthony		1923 Apr 26	1923 May 2	23	4	1329			
Kent	Tina	A.								
Kereluk	Marcin	N.								
Kerr	Lydia	E.								
Kerrigar	John	J.								
Keys	Samiel									
Keyser	Helen									
Kidwell	Annie		1917 Aug 1	1917 Aug 4	25	5	1714			
Kidwell	Lona									
Kieslick	Franz		1934 Feb 15	1934 Feb 21	28	5	129A	M	W	
Kilby	James									
Kilby	Thomas									See: Cain, Patric (Kiley)
Kiley	Thomas									See: Kilby, Thomas
Kilkinny	William	J.	1918 Oct 27	1918 Oct 29	18	4	998			
Kimber	Amos									
Kincade	George		1920 Dec 8	1920 Dec 11	23	2	1568			
Kincheloe	Julius									
King	Eliza									
King	Mollie									
King	Schuyler	E.								
King	Theodosia									
King	Wallace	R.								
King	Willis									
Kingon	Fred		1923 Jul 15	1923 Jul 17	23	4	1332			
Kirbey	Claude	J.	1919 Mar 17	1919 Mar 20	3	10	1765			
Kirby	Mary									

LAST NAME	FIRST NAME	MIDDLE	DIED	INTERRED	SEC.	ROW	GRAVE	G	R	REMARKS
Kirk	Katherine		1933 Jan 12	1933 Jan 17	21	5	1626	F	W	
Kistinor	Andrew		1918 Dec 11	1918 Dec 16	3	10	1769			(Kostinar)
Kitchen	Joseph	S.	1919 May 13	1919 May 17	18	5	1100			
Kitchen	Lelia									
Klocko	Anthony									
Knapeszewska	Gene									
Knapp	Charles		1928 Feb 4	1928 Feb 11	19	3	919			
Knipers	John		1928 Jul 3	1928 Jul 10	15	2	211			
Knolblock	John	P.								
Kobarsho	Glenjua									
Koblosfki	Henry		1927 Oct 17	1927 Oct 24	19	3	910			
Kohr	Harvey									
Kolb	Kenneth									
Kolkotrinos	George									
Konefola	Steve		1933 Nov 25	1933 Dec 1	28	5	142A	M	W	
Konstonopolos	Anostasium		1918 Feb 16	1918 Feb 19	22	4	1297			
Kostinar	Andrew									See: Kistinor, Andrew
Kotterman	Kasper		1918 Oct 30	1918 Nov 2	22	5	1203			
Kotzuba	Seymon									Alias: Leyman Kaitola
Kow	Lirong		1917 Oct 28	1917 Nov 1	3	9	1591			
Kowloufas	Anna	M.								
Kragt	Ludtkos		1928 Mar 15	1928 Mar 24	19	3	922			
Kramer	Charles		1919 Aug 23	1919 Aug 26	15	1	90			
Kratz	Frank									
Kratz	Mary	E.	1934 May 11	1934 May 15	21	4	1504	F	W	
Kratzer	Anthony		1934 May 1	1934 May 8	28	5	118A	M	W	
Kritkis	William									
Kudryk	Koston									
Kuhn	T.	Anna								
Kurtz	Effie		1932 Jan 13	1932 Jan 15	21	1	1606	F	W	
Kutscher	Joseph		1919 Feb 28	1919 Mar 4	18	5	1093			
LaBelle	Alfred									
LaBorie	Henry									
LaCompte	Charles		1935 Jan 31	1935 Feb 7	29	1	150A	M	I	Indian Pt.
Lacy	George	W.								
Lafarrino	Salvatore		1921 Dec 29	1922 Jan 4	23	3	1448			
Lafont	Alphons		1918 Jul 25	1918 Jul 29	22	4	1307			
Lagonesse	William		1934 Nov 18	1934 Nov 21	29	1	158A	M	W	
Lain	Anna		1936 Feb 28	1936 Mar 4	21	4	1280	F	C	

LAST NAME	FIRST NAME	MIDDLE	DIED	INTERRED	SEC.	ROW	GRAVE	G	R	REMARKS
Lake	Sarah									
LaMarr	Ethel									
Lamb	Louis									
Lamont	Donald		1935 Jan 28	1935 Feb 1	29	1	152A	F	W	
Landsart	Gustare		1921 Jul 27	1921 Jul 30	23	3	1440			
Lane	Carrie									
Lanford	Nannie	M.								
Lang	William	G.	1922 Aug 28	1922 Sep 5	15	1	105			
Langley	Edith									
Larker	James									
Larkins	Fannie									
Larson	Cornelius	A.								
Larson	N.		1918 Oct 21	1918 Oct 22	18	4	990			
Latham	Luree									
LaVan	Bertrand		1934 Nov 16	1934 Nov 21	29	1	157A	M	C	Exhumed June 5, 1940.
Lawrence	Omar									
Lawrence	Richard									
Lawson	Kate									
Lawson	Mark	F.								
Lawson	Mary									
Lawson	William									
Leah	Donovan									
Lee	Annie									
Lee	Clarence									
Lee	Cora									
Lee	Etta	L.								
Lee	John		1936 Jun 28	1936 Jul 1						
Lee	John		1937 Aug 20	1937 Aug 25	29	5	279A	M	C	
Lee	Julia		1935 Sep 11	1935 Sep 18	21	4	1267	F	C	
Lee	Laura	B.								
Lee	Lucy									
Lee	Mary									
Lee	Nannie	E.	1936 Nov 16	1936 Oct 10	29	4	255A	F	C	[Death and burial dates possibly reversed.]
Lee	Robert									
Lee	Susie									
Leedy	Helen									
Leftwich	William	L.								
Leigh	Walter	M.								
Lemanski	Annie									

LAST NAME	FIRST NAME	MIDDLE	DIED	INTERRED	SEC.	ROW	GRAVE	G	R	REMARKS
Lemar	L.	Mary	1932 Dec 4	1932 Dec 9	21	5	1624	F	W	
Lenard	Enos									
Lenhardt	Hilda									
Leonard	Harry		1930 00 00	1930 Jan 28	19	5	1132			
Leonard	Mitchell									
Leonberger	Frank									
LeVann	Eleanor	L.								
Levinski	Maurice		1918 Oct 24	1918 Oct 28	22	5	1201			
Lewis	Alice									
Lewis	Editha									
Lewis	Frances									
Lewis	Francis									
Lewis	Herbert									
Lewis	James		1936 Jun 21	1936 Jun 26	21	4	1289	M	C	
Lewis	Jennie		1937 Feb 25	1937 Mar 3	21	5	1168	F	C	
Lewis	John	E.								
Lewis	John									
Lewis	Laura		1918 Sep 10	1918 Sep 14	25	5	1739			See: Luris, Luria
Lewis	Marry									
Lewis	Raymond									
Lewis	Rose		1930 Jul 14	1930 Jul 21	20	5	1143	F	C	
Lewis	Sarah	E.								
Lewis	William									
Librich	Regina									
Liebman	Maggie									See: Lubman, Maggie
Limerick	Delia		1928 Aug 27	1928 Aug 30	20	4	1243			Exhumed; See: McNair, Jane
Lincoln	Charles									
Lindsay	Lucinda									
Linhart	Mesta									
Lipman	Gustar		1934 Jun 3	1934 Jun 8	29	1	172A	M	W	
Lncaster	Louise									
Locke	Queenie									
Locke	Thomas	W.	1920 Feb 2	1920 Feb 7	23	2	1556			
Lockett	Emmett	Elmore								
Lockey	Belle	B.	1935 Feb 8	1935 Feb 12	21	3	1382	F	C	
Loeffler	Joseph									
Lomax	Alexander									
Lombard	Frank		1921 Aug 19	1921 Aug 24	15	1	101			
Lonesdale	Joseph		1919 Jan 12	1919 Jan 17	23	1	1667			

LAST NAME	FIRST NAME	MIDDLE	DIED	INTERRED	SEC.	ROW	GRAVE	G	R	REMARKS
Long	James	C.								
Long	Laura	J.								
Long	Lee									
Long	Thelma									
Longwell	A.	Cadmus								See: Oliver, A. Cadmus
Looney	Mary									
Lopez	Eidth									
Lorett	Mnoy		1921 Dec 18	1921 Dec 27	20	2	1456			(Lovett, Mary)
Lorsen	Hans									
Louis	Edward		1918 Feb 18	1918 Feb 21	22	4	1298			
Louis	Schmitt									
Lovett	Martha									
Lovett	Mary	L.								See: Lorett, Mnoy
Low	Mary	M.								
Lowe	Elizebeth		1928 Mar 14	1928 Mar 20	20	4	1237			
Lowe	Mack									
Lowery	Charles		1935 Sep 13	1935 Sep 19	29	2	177A	M	C	
Lubman	Maggie		1920 Sep 5	1920 Sep 9	20	1	1593			(Liebman)
Lucas	Alice	S.	1920 May 11	1920 May 13	20	1	1591			
Lucas	Jonah									
Lucas	Nannie									
Lucas	Ruth									
Lucas	Sam	C.								
Lucas	Theodore									
Lucas	Thomas		1931 Jun 25	1931 Jun 30	28	2	48A	M	C	
Luckett	Charlotte									
Lund	Helen									
Luris	Luria	E.	1918 Apr 19	1918 Apr 22	25	5	1729			(Lewis, Laura)
Lyles	Amy									
Lymboroplos	Anna		1926 Jul 4	1926 Jul 8	20	3	1350			
Lynass	Joseph		1910 Nov 15	1920 Nov 17	15	1	97			
Lynch	Alfred									
Lynch	Anesta									
Lynch	Charles	H.								
Lynch	Mary	A.								
Lynn	William									
Lyon	Allesta	P. T.								
Lyon	Jonathan		1919 Jun 11	1919 Jun 16	15	1	88			
Lyons	James		1933 Oct 14	1933 Oct 20	28	5	144A	M	W	

LAST NAME	FIRST NAME	MIDDLE	DIED	INTERRED	SEC.	ROW	GRAVE	G	R	REMARKS
Lyons	John	T.	1936 May 1	1936 May 5	29	3	216A	M	W	
Lyons	Osborne	S.	1931 Feb 21	1931 Feb 28	28	2	52A	M	W	
Mabley	John	H.								
Macauley	Christine	D.	1927 Nov 1	1927 Nov 8	20	3	1366			
Mackay	Kalmin									
Mackey	Mary									
Mackie	David		1928 Jun 25	1928 Jul 2	19	4	1005			
MacNair	Jane									See: McNair, Jane
Madden	Thomas		1918 Mar 24	1918 Mar 26	18	3	891			
Madison	William									
Maher	John		1925 Feb 24	1925 Feb 27	23	5	1223			
Mahon	Thomas	R.								
Mahoney	Cecil									
Mahoney	Kate									
Mahr	Frank	X.	1918 Jan 24	1918 Jan 26	22	4	1295			
Maillard	Ernest		1933 Feb 17	1933 Feb 24	28	4	115A	M	W	
Maillet	Jesse		1919 Dec 2	1919 Dec 6	23	2	1554			(Jules)
Maillet	Jules									See: Maillet, Jesse
Major	Stephen									
Mallett	Peter									
Malone	Josephine									
Maloney	Patrick	J.	1917 Nov 15	1917 Nov 19	3	9	1589			
Maloney	Patrick		1932 Dec 30	1933 Jan 5	28	3	62A	M	W	
Manago	Heywood									
Mandley	Madeline									
Mangan	Timothy	B.								See: Manigan, Timothy B.
Manger	Mamie									
Manigan	Timothy	B.	1923 Dec 8	1923 Dec 12	23	4	1337			(Mangan)
Mankins	Sophine									
Mann	Joe		1932 Aug 14	1932 Aug 20	28	3	77A	M	W	U. S. Prisoner
Manning	Thelma									
Manns	Rosa									
Mansfield	Clarence		1919 Dec 27	1919 Dec 31	23	2	1555			(Minifield)
Mansfield	Cornelia		1920 Feb 2	1920 Feb 7	20	1	1588			
Manuel	Francis			1937 Jan 11	29	4	249A	M	W	
Marashlian	Hagopjohn									
Marcel	Walter	G.								
Marchek	Andrew									
Maria	Jose		1918 Aug 4	1918 Aug 8	3	10	1785			

LAST NAME	FIRST NAME	MIDDLE	DIED	INTERRED	SEC.	ROW	GRAVE	G	R	REMARKS
Marion	Edward	B.								
Maritz	Joseph	R.								
Markey	Larence		1918 Jul 21	1918 Jul 23	22	4	1307			(Markey, Lawrence)
Markey	Lawrence									See: Markey, Larence
Markoff	Anna									
Marks	Sarah		1928 Aug 18	1928 Aug 23	20	4	1242			
Marojenic	Theresa		1935 Jan 20	1935 Jan 24	21	3	1378	F	W	
Marriott	J.	A.	1937 Mar 26	1937 Mar 30	29	4	237A	M	W	U. S. Prisoner
Marsella	Isadore									
Marshall	Benjamin		1930 Nov 11	1930 Dec 6	28	2	56A	M	C	
Marshall	Berry									
Marshall	Elizabeth		1930 Sep 14	1930 Sep 20	20	5	1145	F	C	
Marshall	Henry		1918 May 1	1918 May 3	18	3	892			
Marshall	Irene									
Marshall	James		1932 Jul 24	1932 Jul 27	28	3	80A	M	C	
Marshall	John									See: Washington, John
Marshall	Lizzie									
Marshall	Mabel									
Marshall	Mathew									
Marshall	Paul									
Marshall	Richard		1930 Jul 31	1930 Aug 4	28	1	12A	M	W	
Marshall	Stewart									
Martin	Effie									
Martin	Elizabeth									
Martin	Henry	T.								
Martin	John									
Martin	John									
Martin	Leon	M.								
Martin	Samuel		1918 Jul 2	1918 Jul 3	18	4	980			
Martin	Spencer		1917 Jan 25	1917 Jan 30	22	9	1527			
Martin	Walter	Mae								
Martin	Wille									
Mask	Lillian									
Mason	B.	John								
Mason	Edna									
Mason	Lizzie									
Mass	Elbert									
Masselas	Catherine									
Masterson	Blanche									

LAST NAME	FIRST NAME	MIDDLE	DIED	INTERRED	SEC.	ROW	GRAVE	G	R	REMARKS
Matach	Peter		1923 Jan 9	1924 Jan 11	23	4	1338			(Matuch)
Matchett	William	H.	1933 Oct 16	1933 Oct 18	28	5	145A	M	W	D.C. Prisoner
Mathews	Adie	A.	1935 Jan 23	1935 Jan 30	21	3	1379	F	W	
Mathews	Fred									
Mathews	James	B.	1918 Oct 24	1918 Oct 28	18	4	996			
Mathionson	Olav									
Mathison	James	W.	1918 Aug 6	1918 Aug 9	18	4	983			
Matthews	James									See: Matach, Peter
Matuch	Peter									
Mauck	Ellen		1931 Aug 5	1931 Aug 8	21	5	1599	F	W	
Mavers	Mary		1926 Dec 28	1927 Jan 3	29	3	1354			
Maxwell	Rachel		1929 Sep 3	1929 Sep 7	20	4	1265			
Mayberry	Russell	C.	1922 Nov 21	1922 Nov 23	15	1	106			
Mayes	Guy	H.								
Mayhew	Mazie		1932 Aug 4	1932 Aug 10	21	5	1617	F	W	
Mayhew	Rosa	D.	1935 Sep 9	1935 Sep 16	21	4	1266	F	C	
Mayo	Ida									
Mayo	Walter	L.								
McAdams	Regis	W.								
McArdle	Charles	A.								
McAteer	Daniel	J.								
McCafferty	Juidth	Elaine								
McCain	Jasper									
McCarter	Watt									Indian
McCarthy	Nellie	T.								
McCillan	Geraldine									
McClain	William									
McClaren	Robert									
McClinton	Mary	J.								
McCloud	Henry									
McCloud	Lula									
McComb	James		1929 Mar 6	1929 Mar 13	19	4	1028			
McCommick	John		1917 Sep 14	1917 Sep 17	22	3	1417			
McCormich	Edith		1931 Dec 24	1931 Dec 30	21	1	1604	F	C	
McCulloch	William		1922 Apr 12	1922 Apr 17	23	3	1451			
McCullough	Ed									
McCullough	Robert									
McCurry	James		1937 Feb 4	1937 Feb 10	29	4	245A	M	W	
McDonald	Emma									

LAST NAME	FIRST NAME	MIDDLE	DIED	INTERRED	SEC.	ROW	GRAVE	G	R	REMARKS
McDonald	Evelyn		1925 Feb 14	1925 Feb 17	20	2	1470			
McDonald	James	T.								
McDonough	Mary	M.	1928 Dec 9	1928 Dec 13	20	4	1247			Duplicate #; See: Campbell, Lena
McFadden	Virginia									
McGinnis	Arthur									
McGovern	Mary									
McGovern	Thomas		1918 Jul 26	1918 Jul 30	22	4	1210			
McGovern	Walter		1926 Mar 10	1926 Mar 15	10	1	676			
McGrath	John									
McGrath	Sadie		1927 Oct 10	1927 Oct 15	20	3	1365			
McGriff	Richard	F.								
McHenry	Wilson		1937 May 23	1937 May 28	29	5	289A	M	C	
McKenna	Frances									
McKenzie	John	A.	1931 Jun 29	1931 Jul 2	28	2	47A	M	W	
McKeoin	James		1919 Jul 3	1919 Jul 9	23	2	1542			
McKeon	John	T.								
McKesson	Mamie									
McKinney	Herbert		1926 Jan 17	1926 Jan 21	19	1	670			
McKinney	Laura									
McLong	Mary									
McMahon	John	L.								
McMann	Lillian	A.								
McManus	Joe		1926 Mar 17	1926 Mar 19	19	1	678			
McMurray	James									
McMurty	Lewis									
McNair	Jane		1931 Jun 23	1931 Jun 27	20	4	1243	W	F	Alias: MacNair; See: Limerick, Delia
McNally	Charles	Z.								
McOuire	Blanche									
McPherson	Josephine		1934 Jul 8	1934 Jul 14	21	4	1506	F	W	
McPherson	Rose									
McQueen	George									
McRand	John	T.	1936 Jan 5	1936 Jan 5	29	3	217A	M	W	First buried at Arlington National.
McSherry	Smith	B.								
McSweney	Margret		1925 Dec 16	1925 Dec 21	20	2	1477			
McSwyney	Mary	T.								
McWilliams	William		1933 Jan 25	1933 Feb 1	28	3	61A	M	W	
Meadek	William		1917 Jun 29	1917 Jul 2	22	3	1410			
Mealy	Jessie									
Meeks	Margaret		1928 Jan 14	1928 Jan 19	20	3	1367			

LAST NAME	FIRST NAME	MIDDLE	DIED	INTERRED	SEC.	ROW	GRAVE	G	R	REMARKS
Meems	Mary	E.								
Meixell	Elmer									
Menzer	Bert									General Army Prisoner
Mercer	George									
Merchant	William	R.	1935 Aug 10	1935 Aug 14	29	2	180A	M	W	
Mercier	Cyril									
Merritt	Charles									
Merryman	Grace									
Merryman	John	T.								
Mesham	Andrew									
Messett	Patrick		1920 Sep 4	1920 Sep 9	23	2	1562			U.S.P.
Metzger	Joseph									
Meyer	Charles									
Meyers	Althea									
Meyers	Townsend	B.	1929 Aug 21	1929 Aug 27	19	5	1120			
Miagett	Elwood									
Michael	Cahill									
Middleton	Clara									
Middleton	William									
Middough	Baby	Girl								
Miles	Cleveland									
Miles	Hezekiah		1934 Nov 10	1934 Nov 16	29	1	159A	M	C	
Miletich	Rado									Indian
Miley	John									
Millard	Mary									
Milledge	Benny									
Miller	Alexander	D.								
Miller	Charles	E.	1920 May 4	1920 May 5	23	3	1430			
Miller	Emanuel									
Miller	Estelle									
Miller	Florence		1929 Aug 1	1929 Aug 6	20	4	1263			
Miller	Ida									
Miller	Janis	C.								
Miller	John		1936 Dec 18	1936 Dec 24	29	4	252A			
Miller	Matt									
Mills	Florence		1919 Nov 1	1919 Nov 4	20	1	1586			
Mingo	John		1929 Jul 30	1929 Aug 6	19	5	1116			
Minifield	Clarence									
Mininno	Cataldo									See: Mansfield, Clarence

LAST NAME	FIRST NAME	MIDDLE	DIED	INTERRED	SEC.	ROW	GRAVE	G	R	REMARKS
Minor	Andrew	D.	1932 Aug 29	1932 Sep 3	21	5	1619	F	C	
Minor	Fannie		1927 Jan 8	1927 Jan 12	15	2	207			
Minor	John		1921 Feb 25	1921 Mar 1	23	3	1436			
Mion	Louis	L.	1926 Sep 21	1926 Sep 22	20	3	1351			
Mitchel	Clara		1927 Feb 1	1927 Feb 8	19	2	806			
Mitchel	James									
Mitchell	Ellen									
Mitchell	Jefferson									
Mitchell	Joseph									
Mitchell	Raymond	S.								
Mitchell	Rudolph									
Mitchell	Warren									
Mitchell	William									
Mittler	Herbert		1923 Aor 20	1923 Apr 24	15	1	108			
Mixson	Hosea									
Moad	Jessie	B.								
Moeller	Christian		1919 Jul 3	1919 Jul 7	23	2	1541			
Mohatt	Acthur									
Molchanoff	Michael		1936 Apr 15	1936 Apr 20	29	3	219A	M	W	
Mongellnzo	Albert									
Mongo	Mollie									
Monroe	Eugene									
Montgomery	Nathaniel									
Monty	Harry	W.	1918 Dec 4	1918 Dec 7	18	5	1083			
Moody	George									
Moon	Ray									
Mooney	John		1936 Mar 4	1936 Mar 9	29	3	223A	M	C	
Mooney	Kate		1924 Oct 5	1924 Oct 8	20	2	1465			
Mooney	Kate		1924 Oct 5	1924 Oct 8	20	2	1465			
Moore	Della									
Moore	Edna	M.								
Moore	Edward		1937 Sep 4	1937 Sep 13	29	5	275A	M	C	
Moore	Floyd	E.								
Moore	Frank	P.								
Moore	Harriett									
Moore	Harry	M.								
Moore	Jennie		1926 Aug 12	1926 Aug 18	20	2	1467			
Moram	Frank									
Moran	Willard									

LAST NAME	FIRST NAME	MIDDLE	DIED	INTERRED	SEC.	ROW	GRAVE	G	R	REMARKS
Morehouse	Hattie									
Moreland	William									
Morgan	Alice									
Morgan	Charles	J.								
Mori	Katsiyils		1929 Aug 11	1929 Aug 15	19	5	1119			Japanese
Morille	A.									See: Alphonse, M.
Morris	Angelo									
Morris	Ernest		1917 Oct 21	1917 Oct 23	22	3	1420			
Morris	Eula									
Morris	George		1921 Jul 27	1921 Aug 1	23	3	1441			
Morris	William		1934 Oct 16	1934 Oct 19	29	1	162A	M	C	
Morris	Winfield		1917 Aug 15	1917 Aug 17	18	3	877			
Morrison	Catherine									
Morrison	John									
Morrison	Mary	M.	1935 Feb 14	1935 Feb 21	21	3	1383	F	C	
Morrow	Wilson	H.	1921 Dec 7	1921 Dec 9	15	1	102			
Morse	Benjamin		1924 Jul 24	1924 Jul 28	23	5	1211			
Morse	Robert	W.								
Morse	William	L.								
Mortensen	Hans	C.	1930 Jan 13	1930 Jan 18	19	5	1130			
Morton	Fammie	Mae								
Moses	James									
Moses	Rebecca									
Moten	Annie		1935 Jun 10	1935 Jun 13	21	3	1391	F	C	
Moten	George	R.	1926 Nov 23	1926 Nov 27	19	2	797			
Mottett	Rose									
Mowrey	Henerietta									
Moylan	John									
Mucha	Walter									
Mullen	Joseph		1924 Jun 14	1924 Jun 18	23	5	1208			
Mullick	Enasan									
Murphy	Henry	R.	1936 Aug 9	1936 Aug 4	29	3	206A	M	W	[Death and burial dates possibly reversed.]
Murphy	James		1936 Feb 8	1936 Feb 14	29	3	226A	M	W	Alias: Murray
Murphy	John		1923 Nov 8	1923 Nov 13	23	4	1335			
Murphy	Martha									
Murphy	Patricia	J.								
Murphy	Patrick	J.								
Murphy	William									
Murray	Belle									

LAST NAME	FIRST NAME	MIDDLE	DIED	INTERRED	SEC.	ROW	GRAVE	G	R	REMARKS
Murray	Daniel	W.	1925 Mar 23	1925 Mar 27	23	5	1224			
Murray	Edward	L.	1918 Dec 8	1918 Dec 16	18	5	1084			
Murray	George									See: Murphy, James
Murray	James									
Murray	William	H.	1936 May 26	1936 May 26	21	4	1287	M	W	
Murray	William	J.								See: Sixsmith, William
Murray	William									
Murray	William									
Murton	Frank	L.								Army Military Prisoner
Muse	George									
Mustakis	Basil		1918 Aug 22	1918 Aug 18	22	5	1186			
Nabor	Daniel	A.								(Neighbor)
Nalan	Otis									
Naples	Henry		1931 Oct 28	1931 Nov 4	28	2	37A	M	W	
Nardi	Annie	M.								
Narrington	Eleonora		1933 Apr 22	1933 apr 26	21	4	1484	F	W	
Nash	William									
Natt	William									
Natvie	Barclay	Ditalley								
Nauakanic	Nick		1935 Mar 24	1935 Mar 30	29	2	201A	M	W	
Naughton	Helena									
Nauy	M.	P.								See: Pressely, Walter G.
Naylor	Joseph		1920 Nov 6	1920 Nov 9	23	2	1566			
Neal	C.	Ashford								
Neal	Charles	H.								Disinterrred
Neal	Harry									
Neal	Richard									
Neddermeyer	Max	R.								
Negro	Bennie									
Neighbor	Daniel	A.	1926 Nov 29	1926 Dec 2	19	2	798			See: Nabor, Daniel A.
Neilson	Anton									
Neilson	Axel									
Nelson	Charles	H.								
Nelson	George									
Nelson	James	H.								
Nelson	Louis									
Nelson	Ruby									
Nemmore	Joshua		1929 May 23	1929 May 29	19	5	1110			Indian Patient
Nesba										

LAST NAME	FIRST NAME	MIDDLE	DIED	INTERRED	SEC.	ROW	GRAVE	G	R	REMARKS
Nesbitt	Hilda									
Newbury	James		1930 Mar 24	1930 Mar 29	28	1	23A			U. S. Prisoner
Newman	B.									
Newman	Nathaniel		1936 May 9	1936 May 13	29	3	215A	M	C	
Newton	Daniel									See: Nurton, Daniel
Newton	Ella									
Newton	Mary		1918 Feb 19	1918 Feb 23	25	5	1725			
Nichols	Lilly									
Nichols	Nicholas									
Nichols	Peter									
Nickelson	Willie	May								
Nickens	Rubh									
Nielsen	Sophia									
Nightingale	John									
Nixion	Louise	V.								
No Name				1936 Jun 26	21	3	208A			
Noble	Frank									
Nolan	Michael	C.								
Noonan	Charles		1930 Oct 24	1930 Oct 30	28	1	3A	M	W	
Nopolini	Joseph		1936 Mar 1	1936 Mar 5	29	3	224A	M	W	
Nora	Twomey									
Nordun	Ernest		1925 Oct 10	1925 Oct 15	23	5	1234			
Norlon	Thomas	M.								
Norman	Frank		1932 Mar 8	1932 Mar 15	28	2	31A	M	C	
Norris	Goerge									
Norris	Vernon									
Northcott	John		1925 Jun 8	1925 Jun 12	23	5	1230			
Nova	Koveck	Peter								(Newton)
Nurton	Daniel		1924 Jul 23	1924 Jul 26	23	5	1210			
Oats	William		1929 Aug 7	1929 Aug 13	19	5	1117			
O'Beddy	Michael									
OBrien	Charles	H.	1919 Apr 14	1919 Apr 16	23	1	1680			
OBrien	John		1934 Feb 1	1934 Feb 3	28	5	131A	M	W	
O'Connell	John	R.								Military Prisoner
Oconnor	Estelle									
O'Dennell	Mary		1930 Nov 30	1930 Dec 4	20	5	1150	F	W	
O'Donnell	Sarah									
O'Dowd	Seth	E. L.								
Offut	Annie									

LAST NAME	FIRST NAME	MIDDLE	DIED	INTERRED	SEC.	ROW	GRAVE	G	R	REMARKS
Oglin	Virginia		1921 Feb 1	1921 Feb 3	20	1	1597			
OKeefe	Charles	H. O.	1918 Jul 22	1918 Jul 24	18	4	982			
Oliff	Sarah									(Longwell)
Oliver	A.	Cadmus								
Oliver	Clayton	L.	1933 Dec 8	1933 Dec 11	28	5	140A	M	W	Exhumed Jan. 24, 1934.
Oliver	Richard									
Olsen	Fred									
Olson	John		1917 Sep 28	1917 Oct 1	22	3	1418			
O'Neal	Lottie									
O'Neal	Rufus	F.								
O'neill	John		1918 May 2	1918 May 6	18	3	893			
O'Rooney	Patrick		1937 Aug 22	1937 Aug 26	29	5	278A	M	W	
Osborn	John	R.	1923 Mar 12	1923 Mar 15	23	4	1327			
Osny	Denis									
Otemes	James	R.								
Otis	Hugh									
Otis	Isadore									
Otto	August		1919 Mar 12	1919 Mar 15	18	5	1094			
Owens	Arthur									
Owens	John									
Owens	Lillian		1928 Jan 21	1928 Jan 26	20	3	1368			
Owsby	Jesse		1918 Nov 21	1918 Nov 25	18	5	1082			
Oxden	Frederick	D.								
Padden	John	G.								
Page	Elizabeth									
Page	Hattie									
Palerno	Philip		1926 Feb 28	1926 Mar 5	19	1	675			
Palmer	Marion	M.								
Panabaker	Margaret		1933 Jun 4	1933 Jun 9	21	4	1487	F	W	
Papadopoullos	Diamandies		1926 Mar 24	1926 Apr 1	19	1	682			
Pappas	George									
Pararkivas	Pahsinis		1925 May 23	1925 May 28	23	5	1229			(Pathsellis, Paras)
Parent	Norah									
Parish	James	M.								
Parker	Charles	H.								
Parker	Charles	M.	1926 May 23	1926 May 27	19	1	687			
Parker	Ethel									
Parker	John	A.	1936 Nov 28	1936 Nov 27	29	4	254A	M	W	[Death and burial dates possibly reversed.]
Parker	Wallace		1920 Dec 8	1920 Dec 10	23	2	1567			

LAST NAME	FIRST NAME	MIDDLE	DIED	INTERRED	SEC.	ROW	GRAVE	G	R	REMARKS
Parker	William		1932 Jun 26	1932 Jul 14	28	3	81A	F	C	
Parkerson	Robert									
Parks	Margaret									
Parks	Thomas	J.	1927 May 6	1927 May 10	19	3	899			
Parmelee	Rubie		1933 Sep 15	1933 Sep 21	21	4	1493	F	W	
Parrish	Stephens	A.								
Parsons	John	E.								
Pasquan	Dolores		1927 Apr 9	1927 Apr 12	20	3	1358			
Pasquan	Margaret									
Paterson	Karin									See: Peterson, Karin
Pathsellis	Paras									See: Pararkivas, Pahsinis
Patten	Elizabeth									
Patterson	John		1919 Feb 10	1919 Feb 12	23	1	1671			
Patterson	Joseph	J.								
Patterson	Marsha									
Patterson	Mina									
Patterson	Robert									
Patton	Abraham									
Patton	Mary	G.								
Paulelik	Mike		1926 Apr 17	1926 Apr 21	19	1	686			
Paulson	Chris		1932 Oct 17	1932 Oct 24	28	3	71A	M	W	
Paxton	Tula									
Payne	Berther		1928 May 15	1928 May 23	20	4	1240			
Payne	Geetrude									
Payne	Hattie									
Payne	Louise									
Payne	William	C.	1919 Jan 9	1919 Jan 13	23	1	1665			
Payne	William	W.								
Peabody	William	W.								
Peacock	Lula									
Pearbeau	Kearl	M.	1921 Feb 15	1921 Feb 17	23	3	1435			(Perabean, Karl M.)
Pearson	Henry	W.								
Pennington	John	M.								See: Pearbeau, Kearl M.
Perabean	Karl									
Peralto	John									
Perchmer	Joseph									
Perkins	Emma									
Perkins	Julia									
Perl	Julius		1934 Jan 4	1934 Jan 10	28	5	136A	M	W	

LAST NAME	FIRST NAME	MIDDLE	DIED	INTERRED	SEC.	ROW	GRAVE	G	R	REMARKS
Perrine	Ralph	S.								
Perry	Josephine									
Person	Charlie									
Person	John		1930 Jul 31	1930 Aug 7	28	1	11A	M	W	
Pessenger	Bianca	M.								Virgin Islands
Peters	Albertina									
Peters	Stephen									
Petersen	Ralph									
Peterson	Gustave	A.	1924 May 15	1924 May 17	23	4	1341			
Peterson	John		1918 Dec 22	1918 Dec 27	23	1	1664			
Peterson	Karin		1931 Sep 6	1931 Sep 12	20	5	1600	F	W	Alias: Paterson
Peterson	Marie	S.								
Peterson	Mary									
Peterson	Rosalina									Virgin Islands
Peterzala	J.	Mary								
Petton	Charles									
Peyton	Clara	L.	1927 Mar 4	1927 Mar 10	20	3	1357			
Phillips	Charles	Robert								
Phillips	M.									
Phillips	Mildred									
Pickett	Willie									
Pierce	Nathan	L.	1923 Sep 30	1923 Oct 3	3	10	1751			
Pierre	William	L.								
Pinella	Maria									
Pinkney	Gertrude		1937 Jun 11	1937 Jun 15	21	5	1172	F	C	
Pio	Angello		1935 Jan 26	1935 Jan 31	29	1	153A	M	W	
Place	William									
Plunkett	George									
Plunkett	Robert	A.	1919 Jan 17	1919 Jan 21	18	5	1090			
Pogue	Fannie									
Poindexter	Mary									See: Tolliver, Mary
Poletti	Nicola		1932 Feb 27	1932 Mar 4	28	2	32A	M	W	
Pope	William									
Posch	Joseph	J.	1937 Sep 26	1937 Oct 29	29	5	273A	M	W	[Probably interred Sep. 29, 1937.]
Post	Charles	F.	1917 Jul 2	1917 Jul 5	22	3	1411			
Potts	Walter									
Poulson	Annie		1928 Jan 26	1928 Feb 2	20	3	1369			
Powell	Corinne									
Powell	Gertrude									

LAST NAME	FIRST NAME	MIDDLE	DIED	INTERRED	SEC.	ROW	GRAVE	G	R	REMARKS
Powers	Thomas		1933 Aug 1	1933 Aug 3	28	4	93A	M	W	
Prather	Anna		1932 Sep 15	1932 Sep 20	21	5	1620	F	C	
Pratt	John									
Pressley	Walter	G.	1933 Mar 1	1933 Mar 7	28	4	113A	M	W	G. C.; M. P. Nauy
Price	Annie									
Price	Jacob		1921 Apr 22	1921 Apr 25	23	3	1438			Alias: Shirley
Price	John	T.								
Price	Joseph									
Pridgeon	William									
Prince	Elizaeth		1934 Nov 28	1934 Dec 5	21	3	1375	F	C	
Procter	William									
Proctor	Harry									
Proctor	Nicholas									
Prozinski	John		1919 Apr 19	1919 Apr 24	3	10	1761			
Pryor	Robert	E.								
Pryor	Sarah	E.								
Purcell	R.	James	1932 Dec 13	1932 Dec 15	28	3	65A	M	W	
Putnam	Lewis									
Pye	Anna									
Pyne	Harry	C.								
Quareater	Wilson									Disinterred Jan. 30, 1925
Queen	Eugene			1925 Jan 20						
Queen	John		1924 Aug 13	1924 Aug 15	23	5	1212			
Queen	Mary		1930 Dec 5	1930 Dec 11	20	5	1151	F	W	
Queenan	Cora									
Querrard	Augustine									
Querrard	Mathilda									
Quinn	Dennis	F.	1931 Jan 21	1931 Jan 26	28	2	55A	M	W	
Rabbett	Albert	S.	1925 Feb 2	1925 Feb 5	23	5	1219			
Racynet	Philip		1920 Jan 278	1920 Jan 29	3	10	1759			
Radcliff	Larry									
Raeggt	August		1918 Oct 17	1918 Oct 21	22	5	1193			(Roegge)
Ragazzini	Guido		1934 Oct 24	1934 Oct 30	29	1	161A	M	W	Alias: Gydo
Raimes	George									
Raley	John	W.	1925 Jul 11	1925 Jul 15	23	5	1231			
Ramsey	Robert	M.								
Ramstadt	Andy									See: Ramstuck, Andy)
Ramstuck	Andy		1918 Sep 30	1918 Oct 2	22	5	1189			(Ramstadt)
Rasmussen	Enga		1929 Apr 11	1929 Apr 17	20	4	1260			

LAST NAME	FIRST NAME	MIDDLE	DIED	INTERRED	SEC.	ROW	GRAVE	G	R	REMARKS
Rawlings	Ray									
Ray	Ben									
Raymond	Clarence		1918 May 26	1918 May 29	18	4	976			
Raynolds	Alfred									
Readon	Guy									
Reamy	John	B.	1919 Jul 6	1919 Jul 10	23	2	1543			
Rebecco	Earnest		1937 Apr 30	1937 May 5	29	4	233A	M	W	
Rebennack	Sherman									
Redd	John		1920 Sep 10	1920 Sep 14	15	1	94			
Reddick	Reuben	A.	1937 Mar 25	1937 Mar 29	29	4	239A	M	W	
Reddick	Edward									
Reddick	John	T.	1935 Jun 15	1935 Jun 20	29	2	189A	M	W	
Reddistom	William		1933 May 19	1933 My 26	28	4	105	M	C	
Reed	Adolphus	W.								
Reed	Bessie									
Reed	Gertrude		1923 Jan 16	1923 Jan 20	20	2	1461			
Reed	James		1922 May 11	1922 May 13	23	3	1452			
Reed	James									
Reed	Luke									
Reed	Susie									
Reeder	Thomas		1929 Apr 24	1929 Apr 30	19	5	1106			
Reer	Annie	G.								
Rees	Daniel		1934 Jul 22	1934 Jul 27	29	1	168A	M	W	
Reese	Ella	A.								
Reese	George									
Regal	Lucy		1918 Mar 17	1918 Mar 21	25	5	1728			
Reid	Charles		1927 Sep 1	1927 Sep 8	19	3	906			
Reilly	Thomas	J.								
Reimush	George									See: Reininth, George (Reimush)
Reininth	George		1920 May 28	1920 Jun 1	23	2	1557			
Reipschneider	Emil		1926 Apr 24	1926 Apr 28	14	1	115			
Reisinger	William	J.								
Reynolds	John	F.	1931 Aug 6	1931 Aug 11	28	2	42A	M	W	
Reynolds	Mattie									
Reynolds	Noah		1928 Nov 5	1928 Nov 5	19	4	1013			
Reynolds	Norman									
Reynolds	Rachel									
Rheam	Maud									
Rhodes	Eliza									
Rhymer	Louise	L.								Army Prisoner

LAST NAME	FIRST NAME	MIDDLE	DIED	INTERRED	SEC.	ROW	GRAVE	G	R	REMARKS
Rice	James	R.	1937 Jan 31	1937 feb 2	21	5	1166	F	C	
Rice	Valeria									
Rich	Ada									
Rich	Ethel									
Richard	Emmitt	E.								
Richards	Elizabeth									
Richardson	Charles									
Richardson	George		1927 Dec 26	1928 Jan 4	19	3	915			
Richardson	James		1931 Sep 5	1931 Sep 9	28	2	40A	M	W	
Richardson	Joe									
Richardson	Lillie									
Richardson	Lucy									
Richardson	Maggie									
Richardson	Mamie		1931 Jan 25	1931 Jan 31	20	5	1153	F	C	
Richardson	Mary	D.								
Richardson	Walter	J.								
Richardson	Wilbur	G.								
Richmond	Howard									
Ricks	John	W.								
Ridgeley	George		1919 Apr 19	1919 Apr 23	23	1	1681			Alias: Clark
Rigdon	Mabel									
Rigo	Tony		1933 Jun 29	1933 Jul 6	28	4	98A	M	W	U. S. Prisoner
Riley	James	J.	1919 Mar 4	1919 Mar 11	23	1	1676			
Rising Fire	Bessie									Indian
Roberets	Blanche									
Robers	Ennis		1922 Jul 9	1922 Jul 13	23	4	1318			
Roberson	Daniel		1925 Dec 16	1925 Dec 22	19	1	669			
Roberta	Virginia									
Roberts	Edgdar	R.								
Roberts	Marie									
Roberts	Oscar									
Roberts	William	A.								
Roberts	William	J.								
Robertson	George									
Robertson	James	F.								
Robertson	Mary									
Robertson	Maud		1935 Nov 3	1935 Nov 6	21	4	1271	F	W	
Robertson	Robert									
Robertson	William		1918 Aug 12	1918 Aug 15	18	4	984			

LAST NAME	FIRST NAME	MIDDLE	DIED	INTERRED	SEC.	ROW	GRAVE	G	R	REMARKS
Robinson	Alphonzo									
Robinson	Charles									
Robinson	Charles	S.	1918 Nov 12	1918 Nov 16	18	4	999			
Robinson	Edith	M.								
Robinson	Ethel		1932 May 23	1932 May 28	21	5	1614	F	C	
Robinson	George		1926 Nov 13	1926 Nov 19	19	2	796			
Robinson	Henry		1918 May 16	1918 May 18	22	4	1305			
Robinson	Herman		1923 Feb 27	1923 Mar 2	23	4	1326			
Robinson	James	F.	1919 Jul 29	1919 Jul 31	23	2	1547			
Robinson	James		1933 Jun 5	1933 Jun 12	28A	4	103A	M	C	
Robinson	Marcellus	R.								
Robinson	Margaret									
Robinson	Nellie	O.								
Robinson	Samuel									
Rockett	James	H.	1926 Jun 5	1926 Jun 9	19	1	690			
Rocks	Sarah	Kate	1927 Jul 23	1927 Jul 27	20	3	1360			
Roddy	Bernard	A.								
Rodgers	Ella	C.								
Rodier	Andrew		1934 Apr 6	1934 Apr 6	28	5	123A	M	W	
Roegge	August									See: Raeggt, August
Roesher	Bernard	K.	1922 Mar 29	1922 Apr 1	23	3	1450			
Rogers	Henry		1919 Aug 4	1919 Aug 6	23	2	1548			
Rogers	Jennie									
Rogers	Ruth									
Rogers	Solomon									
Rogner	John	W.	1920 Oct 25	1920 Oct 27	15	1	96			
Rollins	Kattie		1930 Nov 2	1930 Nov 8	20	5	1149	F	C	
Rollison	T.	Richard								
Rone	Annie	L.								
Roney	Andrew	J.	1928 May 28	1928 Jun 4	15	2	210			
Rook	Peter									
Rorer	Guy									D. C. Prisoner
Rose	Minnie									
Rose	Nathaniel	S.								
Rosenfield	Nellie									
Rosier	James		1930 May 21	1930 May 24	28	1	19A			
Rosier	Lloyd									
Ross	Hilliard									
Roth	Isaac									

LAST NAME	FIRST NAME	MIDDLE	DIED	INTERRED	SEC.	ROW	GRAVE	G	R	REMARKS
Schon	Alma									
Schoplik	Teckla									
Schropshire	William		1937 Sep 1	1937 Sep 8	29	5	276A	M	W	
Schuldt	Oliver	L.								
Schulte	John									
Schultz	Annie									
Schultz	Thomas									
Schwab	R.	George								
Schwarb	James	S.	1917 Nov 4	1917 Nov 6	22	3	1423			
Scott	Albert	N.								
Scott	Anna									
Scott	Elizabeth	M.								
Scott	Farmer									
Scott	Frank	H.								
Scott	Ida									See: Ida, Scott
Scott	John		1919 Jun 11	1919 Jun 14	18	5	1103			
Scott	Lark									
Scott	Marian									
Scott	Rose	C.								
Scott	Samuel									
Seal	Elizabeth									
Seales	Frank									See: Seals, Frank (Seales)
Seals	Frank	L.	1925 Apr 14	1925 Apr 17	23	5	1226			
Sears	Jessie	H.								
Secherling	John									
Seeberg	Wilhelm		1918 Oct 30	1919 Nov 1	3	10	1773			
Seelback	Herman		1935 Sep 4	1935 Sep 11	29	2	178A	M	W	
Seelhorst	Otto									
Segelarick	Peter									
Sehlamus	Paul									
Self	Rufus									
Selich	John									
Sewer	Frederick									
Sexton	Thomas									
Seymour	John		1934 Nov 11	1934 Nov 14	29	1	160A	M	C	
Shakespeare	Santiago									
Shannon	May	Josephine								
Shaper	Clarice	K.	1937 Oct 10	1937 Oct 15	21	5	1174	F	C	
Sharp	Mary									

LAST NAME	FIRST NAME	MIDDLE	DIED	INTERRED	SEC.	ROW	GRAVE	G	R	REMARKS
Simon	Fannie		1918 Feb 6	1918 Feb 8	25	5	1724			
Simpson	Milton	L.								
Simpson	Stanley									
Sims	John									
Sims	Mary									
Sing	Lee									
Singleton	William	H.	1934 Jun 28	1934 Jul 3	29	1	170A	M	W	
Sitz	Clara		1935 Dec 11	1935 Dec 16	21	4	1275	F	W	
Sixsmith	William		1918 Jan 9	1918 Jan 12	18	3	888			Alias: Murray
Skidmore	Albert	I.								
Skinner	Carrie									
Skinner	Mary	L.								
Slitterdas	Ernest									
Slobodin	Harry		1937 Aug 22	1937 Aug 26	29	5	277A	M	W	
Small	Anna	P.								
Smallwood	Elmer									
Smallwood	William		1918 Oct 22	1918 Oct 24	22	5	1200			
Smith	Albert									
Smith	Anesta									
Smith	Anna		1921 Sep 5	1921 Sep 8	20	2	1455			
Smith	Charles		1919 Jan 20	1919 Jan 23	18	5	1091			
Smith	Donald	E.								
Smith	Eliza									
Smith	Erastus	A.								
Smith	Frank	F.								
Smith	George	A.								
Smith	George	W.								
Smith	George		1919 Apr 29	1919 May 3	18	5	1098			
Smith	George		1921 Dec 21	1921 Dec 27	23	3	1447			
Smith	Harrieet		1926 Dec 7	1926 Dec 13	20	3	1353			
Smith	Jack		1926 Dec 25	1926 Dec 31	19	2	802			
Smith	James	E.	1923 Sep 23	1923 Sep 26	23	4	1334			
Smith	James	F.	1929 Jun 24	1929 Jul 1	19	5	1113			
Smith	John	S.								
Smith	John		1918 oct 22	1918 Oct 23	18	4	991			
Smith	John		1926 Nov 9	1926 Nov 13	19	2	794			
Smith	John									(Colored Man)
Smith	John II		1926 Feb 15	1926 Feb 20	15	1	204			
Smith	Lena		1918 May 27	1918 May 28	25	5	1733			
Smith	Luther	H.								

LAST NAME	FIRST NAME	MIDDLE	DIED	INTERRED	SEC.	ROW	GRAVE	G	R	REMARKS
Smith	Marion	A.								
Smith	Mary									
Smith	Mary	L.								
Smith	Robecca									
Smith	Rosa									
Smith	Rose									
Smith	Sally		1931 Jul 4	1931 Jul 9	21	5	1598	F	C	
Smith	Spencer	D.								
Smith	Thomas (2nd)		1932 Mar 18	1932 Mar 24	28	3	86A	M	W	
Smith	Walter		1920 Oct 15	1920 Oct 19	23	2	1564		W	Alias: Shelkey
Smith	William	W.	1928 May 31	1928 Jun 6	19	4	1004			
Smith	William		1927 Oct 19	1927 Oct 26	19	3	911			
Smith	William		1937 May 22	1937 May 27	29	5	290A	M	C	
Smolinski	George									
Smyniaids	George		1935 Apr 3	1935 Apr 9	29	2	199A	M	W	
Sneed	James		1935 Jul 29	1935 Aug 1	29	2	183A	M	C	
Snow	Sarah		1930 Apr 13	1930 Apr 19	20	5	1140			
Somers	Elizabeth	W.								See: Sumers, Elizabeth W.
Sommerville	William									
Sonna	Yazza									
Sonneis	Jacona		1921 Apr 22	1921 Apr 26	23	4	1316			
Sonneyburg	Hiram		1933 May 7	1933 May 13	28	4	106	M	C	
Soper	Louise		1936 Apr 10	1936 Apr 14	29	3	220A	M	W	Alias: John C.
Southwick	Martha	K.	1924 Jul 7	1924 Jul 9	20	2	1468			
Spalding	William	L.								
Sparks	Sarah	Ann	1921 Jun 29	1921 Jul 2	15	1	99			
Spaulding	John		1917 Sep 11	1917 Sep 14	25	5	1716			
Spearman	Virginia	L.	1932 Feb 25	1932 Mar 2	21	1	1608	F	W	
Spedden	Henry	C.								
Spencer	Shephard		1928 Mar 21	1928 Mar 28	19	4	1000			
Spencer	Virgie									
Spencer	Charles									
Speranega	Stewart		1935 Apr 22	1935 Apr 25	29	2	197A	M	C	
Spetler	Peter									
Spiggs	Henry		1937 Aug 2	1937 Aug 5	29	5	284A	M	C	
Spriggs	Spencer		1935 Jun 6	1935 Jun 17	29	2	190A	M	C	
Spruiell	William		1917 Nov 29	1917 Dec 3	3	9	1587			
St. Clare	William									
Stafford										

LAST NAME	FIRST NAME	MIDDLE	DIED	INTERRED	SEC.	ROW	GRAVE	G	R	REMARKS
Stancil	Toefil									
Stanfield	Julius	W.								Exhumed March 30, 1950.
Stanley	Hugh									
Stanley	Laura									
Stannard	Lucy		1927 Apr 10	1927 Apr 14	20	3	1359			
Staples	Laura	V.								
Stapleton	Inger									Virgin Islands
Statenwest	Carrie									
Stavridis	Madeline	W.								
Steinmyer	Julius		1918 Jun 22	1918 Jun 25	18	4	978			
Stempen	John									U. S. Prisoner
Stepney	Elizabeth	M.								
Sterling	Ella		1931 Mar 27	1931 Apr 1	20	5	1158	F	W	
Stevens	John		1921 Jan 14	1921 Jan 15	23	3	1432			
Stevens	Julia									
Stevens	Louis									
Stevens	Wilhelmina									
Stevenson	John	R.								
Stevenson	Nels		1936 May 18	1936 May 21	29	3	212A	M	W	
Stewart	Charles		1935 Oct 7	1935 Oct 14	29	3	232A	M	C	
Stewart	Daniel									
Stewart	John	C.	1925 Oct 31	1925 Nov 3	23	5	1235			
Stewart	Mary	E.								
Stewart	Mary									
Stewart	Mary		1927 Aug 31	1927 Sep 3	20	3	1362			
Stewart	Norman									
Stewart	Olive	May								
Stewart	Whack									
Stewrt	Arthor									
Stibor	Frank									
Stic	Tony									
Stiles	Skybelle		1936 Sep 12	1936 Sep 14	29	4	261A	M	C	
Stilgerhusby	Vivian									
Stokes	Charles		1928 Sep 3	1928 Sep 10	19	4	1008			
Stoll	Anna									
Stone	William	J.								
Stoop	Henry									
Story	Frances	B.								
Stotts	Marry		1919 Nov 2	1919 Nov 5	20	1	1587			

LAST NAME	FIRST NAME	MIDDLE	DIED	INTERRED	SEC.	ROW	GRAVE	G	R	REMARKS
Stradley	Russell	M.	1917 Dec 7	1917 Dec 11	18	3	883			
Strahle	Bede		1933 Oct 27	1933 Nov 1	21	4	1494	F	W	
Straub	Anton		1935 May 26	1935 Jun 3	29	2	191A	M	W	
Stresner	Theodore		1917 Oct 31	1917 Nov 3	22	3	1422			
Strickler	Edward									See: Stryphon, Emo
Strikes On Top										Indian
Strong	Mary	E.								
Strowtzinsky	Nicholas	N.								
Strozier	Webster		1930 Apr 8	1930 Apr 15	28	12	21A			
Struts	Richard		1925 May 20	1925 May 23	23	5	1228			
Stryphon	Emo		1934 Dec 31	1935 Jan 7	29	1	155A	M	W	Strickler, Edward
Stultz	Vera									
Suit	Emma									
Sullivan	John	O.	1923 May 30	1923 Jun 2	15	1	109			
Sullivan	Lewis	J.								
Sullivan	Michael		1929 May 29	1929 Jun 4	19	5	Blank			Disinterred Nov. 2, 1929
Sullivan	Patrick	O.	1921 Jan 27	1921 Jan 29	3	10	1755			
Sullivan	Robert									
Sullivan	Timothy									
Sumers	Elizabeth	W.	1923 Mar 28	1923 Apr 2	20	2	1462			(Somers)
Sumerville	Flora									
Summers	Edward									
Sun	Long	May								
Suri	Jack									
Surles	Joseph	O.								
Sutton	Willie		1931 May 18	1931 May 25	28	2	50A	M	W	See: Jones, John
Svnelin	Clarence									
Swann	James									
Swann	Mamie									
Swanwell	John		1922 Nov 5	1922 Nov 7	23	4	1320			
Swenney	Thomas		1919 Jan 6	1919 Jan 10	18	5	1087			
Swich	Ely									
Sylvester	Mary	E.	1931 Nov 6	1931 Nov 12	21	1	1603	F	C	
Synder	Isaac		1922 May 28	1922 Jun 1	15	1	103			
Szwedo	Stanley									
Tabbs	Arthur									
Tabler	William									
Tabueno	Fortunato									Filipino [sic]
Taft	Belle									

LAST NAME	FIRST NAME	MIDDLE	DIED	INTERRED	SEC.	ROW	GRAVE	G	R	REMARKS
Talberio	Alfonzo		1919 Apr 7	1919 Apr 9	3	10	1763			
Talty	John									
Tarman	James	E.								
Tate	Alma	E.								
Taylor	Addie									See: Tyler, Addie
Taylor	Bessie									
Taylor	Blanche	W.								
Taylor	Frank									
Taylor	George		1927 Dec 24	1927 Dec 31	19	3	914			Alias: Jones
Taylor	Leslie	E.								
Taylor	Lillian									
Taylor	Margaret	J.								
Taylor	Naomi									
Taylor	Reuben									
Taylor	William									
Taylor	William									
Taylor	Williams									
Tebbe	Erwin									
Teele	Carl									
Temple	James									
Tennyson	Jennie		1929 Aug 29	1929 Sep 4	20	4	1264			
Teodoroff	Jean									
Terarica	Dominico									
Terrell	Robert									
Terry	Annie									
Teung	Lee	W.								
Thomas	Ann		1934 Apr 29	1934 May 5	21	4	1502	F	C	
Thomas	Charles		1917 Jul 4	1917 Jul 6	22	3	1412			
Thomas	Charles		1920 Jul 18	1920 Jul 21	23	2	1560			
Thomas	Charles									
Thomas	Edward	C.								
Thomas	Edward	S.								
Thomas	Eugene									
Thomas	George									
Thomas	George									
Thomas	Henry	C.	1933 Sep 20	1933 Sep 27	28	4	89A	M	W	
Thomas	Ida									
Thomas	James	M.	1934 Mar 30	1934 Apr 5	28	5	124A	M	C	
Thomas	Jane									See: Jackson, Hatie

LAST NAME	FIRST NAME	MIDDLE	DIED	INTERRED	SEC.	ROW	GRAVE	G	R	REMARKS
Thomas	John									
Thomas	Julia									
Thomas	Maggie	V.								
Thomas	Mary	E.	1936 Feb 3	1936 Feb 10	21	4	1277	F	C	
Thomas	Osca		1928 Oct 11	1928 Oct 17	19	4	1010		C	
Thomas	Rosetta	K.	1936 May 1	1936 May 6	21	4	1286	F	C	
Thomas	Sam		1933 Jul 20	1933 Jul 27	28	4	94A	M	C	
Thomas	Susie		1935 Apr 24	1935 May 1	21	3	1388	F	C	
Thompson	Benjamin		1919 May 17	1919 May 20	18	5	1101			
Thompson	Charles		1935 Apr 1	1935 Apr 4	29	2	200A	M	W	
Thompson	Courtney									
Thompson	Eutalia	R.								
Thompson	Gertrude									
Thompson	Henry	T.								
Thompson	Howard		1932 Feb 15	1932 Feb 18	28	2	33A	M	W	
Thompson	Joseph									
Thompson	Mary		1930 Oct 17	1930 Oct 23	20	5	1148	F	W	
Thompson	William	D.								
Thomure	A.	F.	1936 Jul 30	1936 Jul 1	29	3	207A	M	W	
Thornton	Issac									
Thornton	William		1920 Sep 12	1920 Sep 15	23	2	1563			
Thrift	Olivia	M.								
Tibbett	Benjamin		1934 Sep 13	1934 Sep 18	29	1	165A	M	W	
Tibbs	Hamlett									
Tierney	Florence									
Tierney	Joseph									
Tillie	Samuel	O.	1918 Oct 20	1918 Oct 22	3	10	1783			
Tilliman	Charles									
Tillman	Charles	W.	1932 Nov 4	1932 Nov 11	28	3	68A	M	C	
Timberlake	Daisy									See: Timberlake, Deney (Daisy W.)
Timberlake	Deney		1923 Dec 7	1923 Dec 10	20	2	1466			
Timberlake	Wyatt									
Timo	George									
Tintaya	Ricardo									
Tirol	Alyrio		1920 Dec 16	1920 Dec 20	23	3	1431			
Tobas	Ray									
Tobias	Martha	A.								
Todish	Wyed									
Toliver	Bertha		1918 Apr 22	1918 Apr 25	25	5	1731			

LAST NAME	FIRST NAME	MIDDLE	DIED	INTERRED	SEC.	ROW	GRAVE	G	R	REMARKS
Tolliver	Mary									(Poindexter)
Tolliver	Nellie									
Tolso	Martha									
Tolson	Isaac		1930 Jan 9	1930 Jan 13	19	5	1129			
Tong	Yee									
Tonning	Samuel		1924 Jan 31	1924 Feb 5	23	4	1339			
Tonsel	John									See: Tousel, John
Tony	John									
Tooley	Samuel									
Topelius	Vial	A.								
Toppin	Joseph	P.								
Tornie	Fritz									
Torres	Gregoris		1928 Jan 29	1928 Feb 2	19	4	1022			
Tousel	John		1925 Apr 2	1925 Apr 7	23	5	1225			(Tonsel)
Towers	Octavia	A.								
Towet	John		1918 Mar 4	1918 Mar 7	18	3	890			
Trammell	Thomas									
Trapasso	Antonio									
Treadway	Eugene									
Treasher	Anna	F.	1919 Aug 22	1919 Aug 25	20	1	1583			Tree in grave location.
Tree					3	1	1491			Tree in grave location.
Tree							1892			Tree in grave location.
Tree										Tree in grave location.
Trenis	Sarah									See: Trevis, Sarah
Trenno	John		1933 Dec 1	1933 Dec 7	28	5	141A	M	W	
Trevis	Sarah		1918 May 31	1918 Jun 3	25	4	1850			(Trenis)
Trojneck	Joseph									
Trostback	Paul									
Trowbridge	Frank									
Troy	Thomas		1936 Oct 14	1936 Sep 30	29	4	259A	M	W	[Death and burial dates possibly reversed.]
Tsinnyinnie	Mabel		1934 Oct 5	1934 Oct 10	21	3	1372	F	W	Indian; Insane
Tucker	Charles	E.								
Tucker	John	T.								
Tucker	Marie									
Tue	Mun		1937 Feb 17	1937 Feb 23	29	4	241A	M	Ch	Chinese
Turner	Amelia		1926 Apr 12	1926 Apr 15	20	3	1347			
Turner	Bertha									
Turner	Julia		1935 Feb 28	1935 Mar 7	21	3	1384	F	C	

LAST NAME	FIRST NAME	MIDDLE	DIED	INTERRED	SEC.	ROW	GRAVE	G	R	REMARKS
Turner	Laura									
Turner	Louis									
Turner	Mamie									
Turner	Ora			1935 Jan 27	1935 Feb 2	21	3	1380	F	C	
Turner	William	G.								
Turnner	Frank		1929 Nov 23	1929 Nov 30	19	5	1125			
Twaits	Maria		1935 Sep 27	1935 Oct 2	21	4	1268	F	C	
Tyler	Addie									Alias: Taylor
Tyler	Jerry		1926 Oct 17	1926 Oct 22	19	2	792			
Tyler	Maggie									
Tyler	Rebecca									
Tyler	Marie									
Tynes	Elizabeth	M.								
Tyree	Annie	M.								
Tyrell	Louis		1933 Nov 23	1933 Nov 25	28	5	143A	M	W	
Uhlarick	Arthur	W.	1918 Nov 25	1918 Nov 29	3	10	1771			
Ulrich	Kimo		1918 Oct 20	1918 Oct 22	22	5	1197			(Kenro)
Umakara	John	H.								
Underdue	Willie	L.								
Underwood	Mary	A.								
Upshaw	Marie		1926 Jan 29	1926 Feb 3	20	2	1478			Alias: Vetti
Valti	Ernest		1917 Aug 24	1917 Aug 27	22	3	1415			
Van Horn	John		1922 Oct 7	1922 Oct 12	23	4	1319			
Van Hoven	Mary		1932 Apr 29	1932 May 4	21	5	1611	F	W	
Van Pelt	Berton	W.								
Vanderbeck	Vicroire									
Vanderbergh	William									See: Brown, William
Vandyne	Mack									See: Vaun, Mack
Vann	Rita	M.								
Vann	Joseph									
Vargo	Julia									
Varner	Vincenze									
Varri	Mack		1926 Feb 7	1926 Feb 12	19	1	672			(Vann)
Vaun	Savior									
Veals	James		1936 Oct 17	1936 Oct 20	21	5	1163	M	W	
Veitch	Nichols									
Velasquez	Peter									
Venskutnes	Tony									
Venue	Marie									See: Valti, Marie
Vetti										

LAST NAME	FIRST NAME	MIDDLE	DIED	INTERRED	SEC.	ROW	GRAVE	G	R	REMARKS
Vigil	Fidel		1935 Jul 6	1935 Jul 11	29	2	185A		W	Indian Patient
Vill	Valentine	A.								
Vincent	Robert		1923 Jul 2	1923 Jul 7	23	4	1331			
Vistia	Patricio		1922 Aor 1	1922 Apr 4	3	10	1777			
Vlasoff	John									
Von Ferri	Leopold	P.								See: Ferri, Leopold
Vouzik	James	R.								
Waggoner	Theodore									
Wagner	Elizabeth		1919 Mar 10	1919 Mar 13	20	1	1579			
Wah	Sam									See: Wah, Sang
Wah	Sang		1929 May 2	1929 May 6	19	5	1107			Alias: Sam
Wahling	Alvis	H.								
Waites	Russell									
Walden	John	M.	1919 Feb 12	1919 Feb 17	3	10	1767			
Walden	Scott		1928 Jan 27	1928 Feb 2	15	2	209			
Walker	Floreace									
Walker	Jerry	T.	1926 Oct 13	1926 Oct 15	19	2	789			
Walker	John	D.								
Walker	Raymond									
Walker	Richard		1936 Aug 25	1936 Aug 12	15	2	212	M	C	[Death and burial dates possibly reversed.]
Walker	Samuel		1929 Feb 28	1929 Mar 7	19	4	1025			Prob. #1026; See: West, Frank
Wallace	Mamie									
Waller	Oscar									
Walsh	Christopher	F.	1931 Feb 13	1931 Feb 19	28	2	54A	M	W	
Walsh	James									
Walton	Arkola									
Walton	Moses									
Wander	Frank		1928 Jan 7	1928 Jan 12	3	10	1745			
Wang	Chen	Nee								
Ward	Amanda		1933 Aug 30	1933 Sep 5	21	4	1492	F	C	
Ward	James									
Ward	Josephine		1932 Jun 26	1932 Jun 30	21	5	1616	F	C	
Ward	William		1927 Feb 6	1927 Feb 12	19	2	807			
Wardf	Emma									
Ware	Henery									
Ware	Leroy									
Ware	Mry		1933 May 27	1933 Jun 2	21	4	1485	F	C	
Ware	Thomas		1937 Aug 5	1937 Aug 9	29	5	281A	M	C	
Warren	Charles									

LAST NAME	FIRST NAME	MIDDLE	DIED	INTERRED	SEC.	ROW	GRAVE	G	R	REMARKS
Warren	Emma									
Warren	Joseph									
Warren	Mack		1930 Aug 15	1930 Aug 30	28	1	9A	M	C	
Warrick	Sylvester									
Warring	Laura	J.	1934 Nov 20	1934 Dec 21	21	3	1377	F	W	
Warwick	James	R.								
Washington	Anna	M.	1917 Oct 15	1917 Oct 18	25	5	1721			
Washington	Charles		1930 Nov 17	1930 Nov 24	28	2	58A	M	C	
Washington	Franklin									
Washington	George		1933 Aug 3	1933 Sep 6	28	4	90A	M	C	
Washington	George		1935 Mar 20	1935 Mar 27	29	2	202A	M	C	
Washington	Henrietta		1930 Jan 14	1930 Jan 21	20	5	1137			
Washington	John		1923 Jan 21	1923 Feb 1	23	4	1323			Alias: Marshall
Washington	Joseph									
Washington	Robert		1928 Feb 28	1928 Mar 1	19	3	920			
Washington	William									
Washington	William									
Waterman	Harry	A.	1917 Dec 28	1918 Jan 2	18	3	887			
Waters	Albert									
Waters	Mamie	S.	1918 Aug 7	1918 Aug 12	25	5	1737			
Waters	Raymond									
Waters	Rebecca		1936 Oct 16	1936 Oct 20	29	4	258A	F	C	
Watkins	Caroline		1920 May 18	1920 May 20	20	1	1592			
Watkins	James		1934 Oct 7	1934 Oct 11	29	1	163A	M	C	
Watkins	Mary	E.	1917 Jul 28	1917 Jul 31	25	5	1713			
Watley	Emma		1928 Sep 19	1928 Sep 24	20	4	1245			
Watson	Cornelia									
Watson	Henry									
Watson	Irene									
Watson	Mary		1936 Mar 6	1936 Mar 10	21	4	1281	F	C	
Watson	Minger									
Watt	Louis		1926 Jul 8	1926 Jul 13	19	1	695			
Watts	Alexander		1935 Apr 23	1935 Apr 30	29	2	195A	M	W	
Watts	Joseph	S.								
Watts	Winnie	J.								
Weaver	Dora		1928 Feb 10	1928 Feb 14	20	3	1370			
Weaver	Etta									
Weaver	Nora									
Webb	Bernard									(Webster)

LAST NAME	FIRST NAME	MIDDLE	DIED	INTERRED	SEC.	ROW	GRAVE	G	R	REMARKS
Webb	John									
Webb	Laura									
Webb	William		1918 Jul 23	1918 Jul 26	22	4	1308			
Weber	Anitole		1926 Dec 28	1927 Jan 4	19	2	803			
Webster	John	W.								
Webster	Nora									See: Weaver, Nora
Weedon	Annia									
Weeler	William									Interned Alien
Wegner	Beaumount									
Weinard	Joe									
Weldon	William		1932 Oct 25	1932 Nov 1	28	3	70A	M	W	
Wellandsow	Rasmus		1919 Aug 6	1919 Aug 8	23	2	1549			
Wellington	Donovan									
Wells	Andrew		1930 00 00	1930 Sep 6	28	1	7A	M	C	
Wells	Augustus		1936 Sep 4	1936 Aug 29	21	5	1162	M	C	[Death and burial dates possibly reversed.]
Wells	Edward	P.								
Wells	John	H.								
Wenner	Fannie									
Wergley	Milos									
West	Charles									
West	Frank		1929 Feb 19	1929 Feb 25	19	4	1025			
West	Josie	T.	1930 Jun 29	1930 Jul 3	20	5	1142			
West	M.	T.	1927 Apr 14	1927 Apr 19	19	3	895			
West	Parker	J. H.	1928 Nov 22	1928 Nov 22	19	4	1016			
Westerhalt	Adolph									
Weston	Edward		1919 Feb 5	1919 Feb 10	23	1	1670			
Whallon	Jesse	M.	1919 Jan 8	1919 Jan 11	20	1	1572			
Wheeler	Annie		1925 Jul 6	1925 Jul 15	20	2	1447			
Wheeler	Richard									
Wheeler	William									
Wheney	Samuel		1923 Feb 15	1923 Feb 19	15	1	107			(Whinery)
Whinery	Samuel									See: Wheney, Samuel
White	Albert		1933 Feb 15	1933 Feb 22	28	4	116A	M	C	
White	Charles	E.								
White	Charles	T.								
White	Chester	O.								
White	John									
White	Joseph	Edward	1929 Mar 4	1929 Mar 11	19	4	1027			
White	Louise	M.								

LAST NAME	FIRST NAME	MIDDLE	DIED	INTERRED	SEC.	ROW	GRAVE	G	R	REMARKS
White	Marie	G.	1930 Mar 25	1930 Apr 1	20	5	1139			D.C. White Prisoner
White	Mary	V.								
White	Mary	J.	1917 Jul 17	1917 Jul 20	25	4	1857			
White	Onna									Indian
White	Robert									
White	Samuel									
White	Thomas	H.								
Whitecross	James		1920 Feb 15	1920 Feb 18	23	3	1425			
Whitfield	John	H.								
Whiting	Georgia	A.								
Whitley	Zoro									
Whitney	Marcia	R.								
Whittley	Clason	L.	1922 Mar 27	1922 Mar 31	23	4	1317			(Whittlesey)
Whitty	Edward									
Wier	Samuel		1935 Apr 23	1935 Apr 29	29	2	196A	M	W	
Wiggins	Blanch									
Wiggins	Savannah									
Wiggs	Earl	A.								
Wilde	Anna		1918 Dec 28	1919 Jan 3	20	1	1571			
Wiles	Arthur		1918 Oct 22	1918 Oct 24	18	4	992			
Wilhilor	Winter		1918 Jul 7	1918 Jul 9	3	9	1583			
Wilkerson	Abraham									
Wilkerson	Minera	T.	1921 Feb 10	1921 Feb 11	20	2	1453			
Wilkerson	William	L.	1934 Nov 27	1934 Nov 30	29	1	156A	M	C	
Wilkes	Francis	E., Jr.								
William	Carl									
Williams	Albert									
Williams	Bernard									
Williams	Burley		1930 Jun 24	1930 Jul 1	28	1	14A			
Williams	Clarence		1926 Jun 16	1926 Jun 19	19	1	692			
Williams	Cornelius									
Williams	Daniel		1923 Dec 3	1923 Dec 6	23	4	1336			
Williams	David									
Williams	Edward									
Williams	Eladney									
Williams	Elijah		1936 Sep 9	1936 Sep 10	29	3	204A	F	W	
Williams	Elizabeth									
Williams	Emma	J.								
Williams	Frank	E.								

LAST NAME	FIRST NAME	MIDDLE	DIED	INTERRED	SEC.	ROW	GRAVE	G	R	REMARKS
Williams	Goerge									
Williams	Henry	L.	1937 May 27	1937 Jun 3	29	5	288A	M	C	
Williams	James		1918 Mar 30	1918 Apr 1	22	4	1301			
Williams	James									
Williams	James									
Williams	Joseph		1930 Jun 9	1930 Jun 16	28	1	16A			
Williams	Joseph									
Williams	Josephine									
Williams	Julia		1927 Jan 9	1927 Jan 13	20	3	1355			
Williams	kacob	P.	1922 Dec 6	1922 Dec 9	23	4	1322			
Williams	Lee									
Williams	Martha	A.								
Williams	Nancy		1937 Oct 24	1937 Oct 27	21	5	1175	F	C	
Williams	Richard		1918 Dec 19	1918 Dec 23	23	1	1663			
Williams	Robert									Virgin Islands
Williams	Roy									
Williams	Susan		1926 Feb 22	1926 Mar 1	20	2	1481			
Williams	Tosco		1930 Jan 20	1930 Jan 25	19	5	1131			
Williamson	Curtis									
Williamson	Frank									
Williamson	Reginald	M.								
Willis	Henry		1927 Feb 8	1927 Feb 15	19	2	809			
Willis	James	M.								
Willis	Johnnie	A.								
Willis	William		1918 Oct 27	1918 Oct 29	22	5	1202			
Wilmont	George									
Wilre	Louis									
Wilson	Ann									
Wilson	Annie									
Wilson	Arthur									
Wilson	Carrie	A.								
Wilson	Corcia	C.								(Canal Zone)
Wilson	Franklin		1931 Oct 10	1931 Oct 17	28	2	39A	M	C	
Wilson	Fred		1918 Oct 24	1918 Oct 28	3	10	1781			
Wilson	George									
Wilson	Harry									
Wilson	Irvin									
Wilson	James									
Wilson	Jane									

LAST NAME	FIRST NAME	MIDDLE	DIED	INTERRED	SEC.	ROW	GRAVE	G	R	REMARKS
Wilson	Joseph	M.								
Wilson	Lela									
Wilstack	Cora	E.								
Windborn	Sam		1921 May 20	1921 May 24	23	3	1439			
Winfield	Frank		1919 Jan 21	1919 Jan 24	23	1	1668			
Winfield	John	H.								
Winkelman	Blanch		1918 Nov 9	1918 Nov 14	22	5	1205			
Winkler	Frederick									
Winnick	Klem	K.								
Winters	Michael									
Winters	Mosby		1933 Jun 30	1933 Jul 7	28	4	97A	M	C	
Wise	Bruce									
Wise	Hattie									
Wiseman	Mary		1932 Oct 9	1932 Oct 15	21	5	1622	F	C	
Wisnawski	Vincent									
Withers	Clyde									
Wittenberg	Franz		1921 Nov 19	1921 Nov 23	23	3	1445			
Wittey	James									See: Hoke, James
Wo	Wang	V.	1926 Feb 16	1926 Feb 19	19	1	673			
Wolf	May									
Wolfe	Samuel		1920 Aug 2	1920 Aug 5	23	2	1561			
Wolfes	Louis	R.								
Wong	Fu	Kui								
Wood	Eleanor									
Wood	Frederick	L.								
Wood	Joseph									
Wood	Josephine	E.								
Wood	Parcker		1936 Apr 17	1936 Apr 22	29	3	218A	M	C	
Wood	Robert	A.	1929 Jul 28	1929 Aug 1	19	5	1114			
Wood	Russell		1917 Aug 1	1917 Aug 3	22	3	1414			
Wood	William	D.	1925 Feb 4	1925 Feb 6	23	5	1220			
Woodfolk	Bessie									
Woodson	Hattie									
Woodup	Alphonsine									
Woodward	Clide									
Woor	Victor		1920 Jul 7	1920 Jul 10	23	2	1559			
Wormley	Fitzhugh		1918 Dec 13	1918 Dec 17	23	1	1661			
Wormley	William		1932 May 31	1932 Jun 6	28	3	83A	M	C	
Wrens	Michael		1918 Oct 26	1918 Oct 31	3	10	1775			

LAST NAME	FIRST NAME	MIDDLE	DIED	INTERRED	SEC.	ROW	GRAVE	G	R	REMARKS
Wright	Granville	M.	1933 Feb 10	1933 Feb 14	28	3	60A	M	W	
Wright	Harry									
Wright	John									
Wright	Nannie									
Wright	Ralph									
Wright	Richard									
Wright	Thomas		1937 Oct 9	1937 Oct 15	29	5	270A	M	C	
Wright	Winston									
Yancy	Robert									
Yankevitch	Paul									
Yantis	Ida	M.								
Yates	Elijah		1932 Oct 18	1932 Oct 22	28	3	72A	M	W	
Yates	Elizabeth		1935 Jan 29	1935 Feb 6	21	3	1381	F	C	
Yazzie	Hoskee		1936 Mar 11	1936 Mar 16	29	3	222A	M	I	Indian
Yick	Lin									
York	John		1937 Dec 23	1937 Dec 30	15	3	320	M	C	Disinterred July 30, 1940.
Young	A.	Simms								
Young	Carson									
Young	Dora									
Young	Ella	E.								
Young	George	E.								
Young	Leon	A.								
Young	Lindsay	P.								
Young	Lottie	M.								
Young	Lucy									
Young	Maria									
Young	Mary	A.								
Young	Thomas									
Zacharais	Socrates									
Zacharias	Anthony									
Zachavides	J.		1918 Feb 19	1918 Feb 23	22	4	1299			U. S. Prisoner
Zaishoff	Charles									
Zalph	Anna	S.								
Zaugg	Gattfried		1937 Jun 28	1937 Jul 6	29	4	246A	M	W	
Zimmer	Alexander									
Zimmerman	Antonio									
Ziska	Joseph									
Zivan	Z.	Sivchev								
Zmukeher	Adulf		1917 Oct 5	1917 Oct 8	3	9	1593			

LAST NAME	FIRST NAME	MIDDLE	DIED	INTERRED	SEC.	ROW	GRAVE	G	R	REMARKS
Zuara	Joseph									Indian
Zuna	Francis									
Zunich	Samuel									
Zuppa	John									

Made in the USA
Monee, IL
24 February 2023

28554317R00050